The Extra Parent

Also by Elaine Denholtz

Plays

Frozen
The Dungmen Are Coming
Hey Out There, Is There Anyone Out There?
Some Men Are Good At That
The Highchairs
Love Games
Doggy Bag

Films

Summerhill
Waiting…The Life Styles of the Elderly
The Dental Auxiliary
What's Inside
Is That What You Want For Yourself?
Another Mother (Eugene O'Neill adaptation for television)

Books

Education, Where It's Been, Where It's At, Where It's Going (contributor)
The Highchairs
How To Save Your Teeth and Your Money (co-author)
The Dental Facelift (co-author)
Having It Both Ways
Playing For High Stakes
Balancing Work and Love
The Zaddik: The Battle for a Boy's Soul

The Extra Parent

✦

How Grandparents Are Helping Out, Pitching In, and Raising Their Grandchildren

Elaine Denholtz

iUniverse, Inc.
New York Lincoln Shanghai

The Extra Parent
How Grandparents Are Helping Out, Pitching In, and Raising Their Grandchildren

iUniverse, Inc.

For information address:
iUniverse, Inc.
2021 Pine Lake Road, Suite 100
Lincoln, NE 68512
www.iuniverse.com

ISBN: 0-595-30400-1

Printed in the United States of America

In loving memory of my parents

Lillian Sachs Grudin, superlative grandmother

and

Maurice Grudin, extraordinary grandfather and great-grandfather

- Research for this book was supported by a generous grant from *The Wallerstein Foundation for Geriatric Life Improvement* and assistance from Fairleigh Dickinson University.

Contents

Foreword

Millions of grandparents are acting as part-time or full-time parents. Some for reasons of drugs, mental illness, incarceration, abandonment, or death of the parent. And some because the parent is unable or unwilling to raise their child. Into this breach steps the grandparent.

The true stories you will read explain the circumstances of grandparents' involvement with their grandchildren—a social phenomenon which has largely gone unnoticed by social commentators and policy makers. In the past twenty-five years, the increased vitality of grandparents and the rising needs of parenting have created a unique resource. The previous generation is caring for the next generation.

Grandparents offer stable, loving homes to millions of children who are at risk. For others, grandparents offer a second set of hands and support to working parents. In every situation, the unconditional love of grandparents is there for their grandchildren. It heals, it cures, it creates miracles.

The moving portraits you will read describe this miraculous bond, documenting the powerful effect grandparents have on their grandchildren.

Gerard Wallace, Esq., Director
Grandparent Caregiver Law Center, Brookdale Center on Aging

Bigette Castellano, Executive Director
National Committee of Grandparents for Children's Rights

1

DIFFERENT KINDS OF GRANDPARENTS

You're a grandparent. You want to do everything right for your grandkids. See them grow and thrive, be healthy and confident. Maybe you're even helping your daughter or son raise your grandchildren. You baby sit, you keep them, or you mind them on a regular basis. Sometimes it feels good and sometimes it doesn't.

There are so many different kinds of grandparents and each situation takes different skills.

- Are you a grandparent living with your grandkids in *their* home?

- Does your daughter or son drop them off at *your* home?

- Do you go to their home *on a regular basis* to help out?

- Do your grandkids *live far away,* so you phone and visit and send birthday gifts, keeping in touch as best you can?

- Are you a *step-grandparent?*

- Are you a *working* grandparent?

- Are you a *retired* grandparent?

- Do you do your grandparenting on an *unstructured basis,* working it out according to what comes up?

That's what this book is about. **How grandparents are reinventing the three-generation family**. How they cope. What works and what doesn't work. This book does not give legal, medical, or financial advice. What it does is offer you true stories of grandparents, just like yourself, who are pitching in, helping out or even raising grandkids. You'll hear about their gripes and their joys. Their frustrations and their successes. The bumpy roads they've traveled and the problems they've solved.

When you read these stories, you'll hear echoes of your own life as a grandparent. And even though some stories are different from your own experience, they will still leave a mark. Why? Because every story has the ring of truth. These are real people, not statistics.

A sad story about a grandmother forced to take over because her daughter has died. A happy story about a grandmother who is thrilled to be needed and comes to her daughter's home on a regular basis. An amazing story about a grandfather who left Taiwan to become his daughter's nanny in New Jersey.

Most grandparents feel deep and loving ties to their grandkids. But let's face it, sometimes it can be hard work. Even if you take care of your grandkids on a temporary basis or a part-time basis, **that doesn't mean you never get tired, frustrated, and inpatient. Every grandparent does.**

In this book you'll meet ten grandparents who are white, black, Hispanic, and Asian. Eight are *grandmothers* and two are *grandfathers*. Some are rich, some poor. Some young, some old. Some retired, some working. They tell you what it's like to walk in their shoes. And sometimes you'll recognize yourself and nod your head. You'll know you're not alone.

These grandparents offer not only their stories, but also their own **SMART TIPS**, the coping skills that work. How to get past the bad times. How to tap into your own physical and emotional strength. How to do the job well. How to be a wonderful grandparent and spend valuable time with your grandkids. This book is about living your life as a grandparent. How to enjoy it more fully, be more effective, and feel more satisfied.

Okay. Let's get started.

How Do You Interact With Your Grandkids?

Grandparents have different attitudes and different experiences. Different incomes and different ages. Different health problems and energy levels. So naturally, everyone interacts differently with their grandkids.

According to *The AARP Grandparents Survey* done in 1998, about "11% of mature grandparents are caregivers." Mature means over fifty years old. But I know grandparents under fifty, don't you? So I'm guessing that number is really higher than 11%. Four out of five caregivers are *grandmothers*.

Enough about numbers. What kind of relationship do you have with your grandkids? Are you their baby sitter, friend, or advisor? What do you buy them? Is it fun taking them shopping at the mall? Going to the movies? Going to church or synagogue with them? Do you watch TV together? What values do you pass on to them? Do you have arguments about the best way to handle situations? How do you discipline them? Do your grandkids and their parents appreciate what you do? Do you expect respect?

Do you resent not hearing from them often enough? Do they expect too much from you? How do you say *no* when you can't do what they ask? Do you ever feel guilty or depressed about being a grandparent?

As you read these stories, think about your own situation. If you're like many other grandparents (31%), you probably phone or visit often, maybe weekly. If you're a grandfather in his fifties, you probably use the internet to keep in touch. What's the most popular activity grandparents do with their grandkids? Eating! Eating out or having a meal together at home is the most common activity grandparents share with their grandkids.

Read these stories and compare them to your own experience. Maybe you don't agree with some of their ideas. Or maybe you'll discover new ideas that speak to you. At the end of each story, you'll find the grandparent's **SMART TIPS.** Do you agree with them? Which ones make sense to you?.

When you get to the end of this book, you'll find a blank page for you to make notes. Write down a page number or a particular story you want to go back to. Or a thought you have. Or a reminder about something you want to do with your own grandkids. Jot down whatever comes to mind. Loving our grandchildren motivates us. But coping skills help us do our grandparenting smarter and better.

This book shows you how grandparents are interacting with their grandkids in positive ways. You can too. Take a look at **Resources and Organizations** at the end of this book which lists places that can help. Look over the **Bibliography for Further Reading.** Good luck!

Okay, it's time to meet **Alice.**

2

ALICE

❖

She was a Young, Unmarried Mother

Some grandparents have no choice about raising their grandkids. A crisis forces them to become parents again, and this can be really tough. Maybe they're older and have medical problems of their own. Maybe arthritis has set in and at sixty or seventy they can't bend very well to tie a child's shoelace or sweep a child off a swing.

If money is tight and they're living on Social Security checks, that's another challenge. The extra household and childcare chores remind them that their energy level is not what it was when they were raising kids at twenty-five or thirty.

Yes, the world has changed dramatically and parenting has changed too. So they feel overwhelmed. The crisis that *forced* them to take over can lead to depression, shame, and humiliation. How can they become parents again? How can they keep going in the face of such obstacles? How can they cope?

In this chapter, you will meet **ALICE**, a grandmother who *could have* folded up and sunk into mental depression when she learned that her unmarried daughter was pregnant. Why didn't she? What kept her on track? How did she manage?

"I made up my mind I'm gonna see my grandson grow up!"

ALICE, 54, is a light-skinned black woman with salt-and-pepper hair and a cheerful disposition. "C'mon in." She unlocks the front door to the enclosed porch and I see stickers all over the place warning that her little, yellow frame house is protected by ADT. It's a rough neighborhood. "They broke in twice, took my watch and a CD player and a little TV. I pay $52 a month for protection."

I follow her into her small, neat kitchen. It's eight a.m. and she's already got a pot of chicken wings on the stove. We sit around her dining room table and she brings me a mug of coffee. She is the mother of one daughter, 33, and she has a grandson, 13. No one else is at home. Her second husband and daughter are both out working.

Alice is a woman comfortable with herself. She is comfortable in her house and comfortable in the oversized white t-shirt and black sweats she's wearing. She peels the paper off her corn muffin and takes a bite. "Mmm, good." She licks her fingers. "Sure you don't want one?"

"My grandmother raised me and my sister until I was 13 and she was 9. I was 41 when my grandson was born. [He came] two days before my birthday. I was working as a switchboard operator in Newark. The baby's father was not [my daughter's] husband, so she was faced with raising a child alone. He was born in distress, a C-section. They were young. So I said, 'I'll pitch in as much as I can. I'll take off and stay home with my grandson.'

My husband is a mechanic, he was the breadwinner, head of the house. So [we] made the decision, and my daughter and the baby's father were satisfied. She went back to work and I kept the child. It was fun. We bonded. And it's still a connection there today. I'm his second mom, we have that closeness. He'd wake up in the morning and grandma was right there, like he was waiting for me. I got his bottle, we went for walks, we had a good time. I loved it. I really, really did.

I like to feel needed, I do. Right! If I can pitch in, even if I don't know the person, it's in my heart. My grandmother raised us to love one another. I was Methodist then, now I'm Baptist. We had to go to church two, three times a day. So I had that foundation: my grandmother and my religion.

Did my husband object? No. I gave them equal time. The daytime was for my grandson, the evening was for him. When she came in from work, my daughter took over her motherly duties. We didn't have arguments. My daughter prepared his bottles and gave me the schedule. I followed the directions. The love and nurturing, it came from my heart. It made it very easy.

My grandson is thirteen now, taller than his grandmother. If he gets mouthy, all I have to do is *look*. I give him a look and that's it! Discipline? When he was young, we had a little bush in the front, we called it *some switch* T. You don't do something right, you get a little switch T on your legs and you know to stay in line. It was very good. We cut off a little branch. That's what my grandmother did to me. I instilled it in my daughter the same way. He sees the switch, and he's frightened. I say, 'go get a piece' and he knows it hurts. Between me and my daughter, we work together. I'm a team player anyway. No resentment, none whatsoever, none. I felt I was *supposed* to do it. I see a stray cat, I'm gonna feed it.

We're borderline financially. We're never on welfare, no. We satisfy our needs and our bills. [Only] one month when I moved from Philly to New Jersey, I applied for public assistance and they gave me $122 and $10 in food stamps, and I found me a job and I said, 'Thank you, I no longer need it.' And it was a stepping stone for me. One good thing is I took up Early Childhood. I got my certificate from Essex County College. I did this for me, this was for me.

With me working and my husband and daughter working, we manage to make ends meet. Oh, we had rough times in the winter cause of the oil, so we pitched in monies. 'It's your turn.' My husband had the bulk, so my daughter and me, we took the small load. We cut back. We go to the food store, we get the basics, not junk food. I make a cake and cookies for sweets.

School was in our backyard. I'd be hanging the clothes on the line, he'd be changing classes and yell, 'Grandma, make a cake.' It was a treat, cake and cookies. He'd yell, and I'd be throwing kisses. My grandson was happy. No Toys-R-Us, no, no, no. He'd come home from school and I'd say, 'Guess what I got for you.' And he'd say, 'I smell something.' It was a treat.

We have medical problems. My grandson, he has asthma, so does my daughter, asthma's hereditary in my family. I don't have it, [but] I'm a diabetic, I have daily medication. We have bills for the asthma, she takes care of those. And [when] I was office manager in a health facility, it helped us out a lot. The people gave us [free] samples. I had health insurance through my employer. I don't have it now, I have it through my husband, and my daughter has it through her employer, The Jewish Community Center.

Did I get tired? Exhausted? I don't know where I got the strength from. It comes from within, God given strength. I was 41 and I always said, 'I'm gonna make it.' I'm a survivor. [Sure] there were dark times. When I was sick, I thought I'm gonna be a burden on everybody. I had surgery, I had colon cancer in 1990. My grandson was three years old. *But I made up my mind I'm gonna see him grow up.* Yes, yes, yes. And this year, my doctor said everything was clean and most times after ten years, you have beaten the cancer. It was kinda scary. I was saying, 'Hey, I didn't put it there. Only God can remove it.' I got a lot of faith. Strong. Strong.

Who's responsible for my grandson now? If I get a call from the school he's sick and I'm here, I go. If my daughter's not at work, she goes. Whoever is closest. We give both numbers, hers and mine. We have a backup, stepbrothers and friends. The father pays child support, he has another family now. But my grandson is his only boy, and he's getting older and asking, 'Hey, where's my father?' So he's taking time with him.

Discipline? Stress? I let my grandson talk it out. He keeps a lot of things inside him. He talks with his mother, she's like a big sister, and they have a good rapport. I always told him to be honest with himself and let your feelings out because it'll make you sick. You let it out and you feel better. We talk about what causes stress. You don't carry grudges, it only makes you feel bad. You don't give it no mind. I gave him a strong background like my grandmother did us.

Problems? We pitch in. The first time, I was laid off and I was sick and how am I gonna make it? And the support was given to me by my daughter and my husband. They took over everything before my disability kicked in, and we made ends meet. I don't know where [the money] came from. They did everything, everything paid on time: electricity, gas. And I felt bad I couldn't contribute. And I was told, 'you can't do it, we'll handle it.' And they did. We're a family with a lot of pride.

What do I worry about? Well, my grandson, he's doing well. What I worry about is I don't want him to get with the wrong crowd. He picks his friends and he has very few friends. And I say, 'Sit back and observe.' And he does. And his mother instills in him not to hang out with, well…There's people who hang out on the street corners. He's not smoking yet, no, not that we know of. I used to smoke before I had my surgery, and my daughter can't [with her asthma]. So he's aware of the danger.

Drugs, that's the worst. In our community, you could ride in any area and see the drugs. It's so prevalent, you have to instill in the child, say, 'You want to be like that?' Out there on the street [it's bad]. 'Is this the life you want to live? No. You want to get yourself an education, what you got nobody can take away from you. So learn all you can, while you're young. And apply it. Use it. Don't get hung up in the wrong crowd. Go the opposite direction.' Say, 'I'll see ya,' and keep moving.

He had some friends and we said [to him], 'You see which way Jason is going? You want to be like that?' We didn't threaten, we let him wean himself away. How? [Gave him] chores to do at home. Bought him games to play. Now this other child is in some kind of "boot camp" for stealing cars. They call it boot camp because they really give them the boot. He knows it's his choice and he knows right from wrong, to choose his friends selectively.

My mental health? How do I stay calm in a crisis? It was the hardest time when my mother passed. I had to get everything together, I still have a lot of loose ends. She had a little home in Philly, which I'm never going back to live [there]. See, we own this home, the mortgage is finished. It's one family, seven rooms and a finished basement and a nice yard.

When I was growing up, I said, 'I'm gonna live in a yellow house on top of a hill.' And one day I'm sitting in my back yard having a cookout, and I look up and there it is, my yellow house, and I said, 'I got my wish, I got my dream!' How many people get their dream? It happened to me. Yes, I made it happen, I did.

Money? I'm working two jobs now. Yes, I am, yes, I am. The first job, I get up at five o'clock in the morning, yes, I do. And I'm on the job six o'clock. And I'm done nine. I leave [the first job], I drop by home just to check the alarm's on or put on a pot, like turkey wings. And my daughter, she'll take over when she gets home from work, it'll be in the oven. [Then] I go off to the second job. It's only seven minutes up the hill. I'm an assistant day care teacher at Christ Church. I teach two-and-a-half to three-year-olds. Very busy, they'll be jumping off the walls. High energy, definitely. I have eleven in my group I'm responsible for. I start at ten and I stay until six. A long twelve hour day.

But I like what I'm doing, so it's not stressful. And my husband gets home before me and he will pitch in, and my daughter will pitch in. It's team work. She'll do the meat part, and he'll fix the vegetable part, and dinner is done. I come in. I wash up. I wind down and put on my gown and lay back and look at the news.

And I love Jeopardy! My grandson does too. And Wheel of Fortune.

Now he's thirteen, he hangs with his grandpa. They get in the car and they go to Home Depot. He says, 'I'm leaving you women alone and I'm going with Grandpa.' Home Depot is their second home, and they buy materials to build things. And he does his chores. Take for instance, snow days. My husband is thinking maybe he'll get the boy next door, and [when] he comes home, my grandson, he has it all done. And my husband says, 'Man, you saved my life.' So he paid him and said, 'Now you're gonna start a bank account.'

My grandson, you don't have to ask him. He sees things need to be done, he does it. Like the kitchen, he scrubbed down the floor, wiped down everything. I have to give him credit. No threats. No switch T anymore. No, no, no.

Power struggles? If he doesn't do his school work, his mother reprimands him. She'll take away a game. If we don't agree on the discipline, we don't argue in front of him, no, no, never. We look at each other. That look, *I still have that look*, I give her a look that means no, don't do it, it's wrong. And she knows it means I'm serious. They know don't mess with [Alice]. We know we have to work together. We let each other know where we stand.

The thing is if my grandson said, 'You can't tell me what to do, you're not my mother,' well that look does it all. We don't let him be disrespectful, oh no, no, no. You'll never be old enough to say certain things to us, it's not allowed, it's not allowed. He wouldn't be standing here if he ever swore at me, no, no, no. We're not going that route. I have to say he has great respect.

Where'd he get it from? He just knows within [what] not to do. I'll be talking *to* him, not *at* him. I say, 'Listen, you know right from wrong.' Not screaming at him. 'You better do this or that!' I say, 'I want this done this way. Okay?' And I explain it. There's no such thing as, 'I don't want to do it.' We're the boss. He's still a child. We're the adults.

But you have to listen, let him explain his reasons to know what's going on inside himself. [If] a storm's going on in him, then okay, I [want to] know what he doesn't want to do and why. His reasons.

I'm so proud of this grandson. My pride came from Day One, he was so manageable. Even when he's away from home, I don't have to worry he's going to tear up somebody's house. No, no. He respects his toys, so he knows how to respect others'. If you have that self-respect instilled, you can respect others.

I say, 'Hey! He's coming out right! Maybe we did something right!'

I have step-grandchildren too, and I want them to get all the schooling they can, go to college. I say to my grandson, 'Go into computers,' because he knows a lot about electronics. Something's broke? He flips it over and fixes it. I was that way. Just using common sense to figure it out. His goal is college. He's happy. Not just me pushing him.

Tips for grandparents raising their grandkids? Be patient and stay focused on what they're doing at all times. Don't let your guard down. Keep yourself in tune. I have to pamper me, too. Massaging my feet. Watching Jeopardy. So far my grandson is beating me, so I have to brush up.

Am I ever taken for granted? No, no, no.

Just never use that word *can't*. Say, 'I can, I can!'"

ALICE could easily have sunk into depression. Yet she never complained or heaped blame on her daughter. Instead, she took over the job of raising her grandson with confidence and good will. At 41, she was a very young grandmother. Her attitude was upbeat.

Why does Alice succeed when others, in her circumstances, fall apart? What qualities give her strength?

SMART TIPS FROM ALICE

Use your religious foundation and your faith to help you stay strong.

Don't be resentful. Accept that you are supposed to help your grandchildren.

Be patient. Stay focused. Never say, 'I can't.' Say, *'I can, I can.'*

Instill self respect in your grandchildren. Encourage them to go to college.

When illness strikes, accept help from your family if they can pitch in.

Listen to your grandchildren, let them explain their reasons.

Don't carry grudges.

Show your grandkids, by example, that you're a family with a lot of pride.

Work hard to pay your bills. Be a team player on household bills and chores.

Discipline your grandkids. Let them know that adults are the boss.

Do nice things for yourself. A foot massage. A favorite TV show.

Get an education. Earn a college degree and work in an area you like.

Encourage your unwed daughter to work and contribute as best she can.

When money is tight, no junk food, no Toys-R-Us. Bake treats as rewards.

Show your grandkids that poor choices, like drugs, can destroy them.

Don't threaten. Help your grandkids to talk out their feelings.

Have fun with your grandkids. Play games with them. Watch TV together.

Show your grandkids that everyone in the family works and works together.

Don't argue about discipline in front of your grandchildren.

Let your grandchildren know your family has values and standards to uphold.

Give your grandkids chores to do. Encourage them to contribute to family life.

Take pleasure in your grandkids' accomplishments.

Be grateful for what you have, any dream that comes true.

Let your love come from your heart.

In the next chapter, you will meet another grandmother. Her motivation for taking care of her two grandsons is wildly different from Alice. So are her circumstances. **BETTY** drives two or three times a week to her wealthy married daughter's home where a live-in housekeeper does the cooking and cleaning.

She doesn't *have* to do this, she *wants* to. And she tells you why.

3

BETTY

✦

To Enrich Them

When a grandmother drives to her daughter's home three times a week to look after her two grandsons, you know she has her reasons. Particularly when her daughter's salary looms well over a million dollars a year, and the family lives in an elegant home run by a trusted housekeeper. No money problems in her daughter's home, no health problems, no visible signs of discontent. Plus a son-in-law who is a good dad and a supportive husband.

Then why is this grandmother so intent on this? What is her mission? Blessed with good health and a fine husband of her own, shouldn't this retired schoolteacher be enjoying a well-earned lifestyle of relaxation? Why does she choose to spend so much time with her grandsons, ten and eight?

To this grandmother, it all makes sense. Because "wealthy" does not spell "wonderful" to her. She wants much more for her grandsons and she explains why.

BETTY, 70, is a pretty, petite, ash blonde wearing a smart pastel blue pants suit and a welcoming smile. Her suburban split level home is warm and inviting, a house built in the fifties with books, magazines, and plants. We sit down at her dining room table and, like Alice, she brings me a mug of coffee.

"When my daughter was made a director of her company, one of the things they said was, '*We know you have a good support system.*' They meant a very good nanny who's been with them over ten years. And [she had] me and my husband. For her promotion, she'd have to be away from home a lot, she'd be traveling. She's competing with men. Only five women directors and 200 men worldwide. She's making over a million a year.

It's a lot of travel, but she tries to be home at night [even] if it's very late. Or she could be going to Europe for three or four days. Her husband has gone into his own business, they spend a lot of time in their fields. I wanted to help them with the children.

I retired from teaching three years ago. I started helping [even] before my retirement. I'd go once, twice a week. But now the boys are in higher grades, especially the older one. He gets a tremendous amount of homework. And they're busy with Hebrew school and soccer and basketball and a scrabble club and a chess club. They need more help in the daytime hours when the parents aren't home. Even on a good day, she may not get home until seven or eight and it could be much later. She has a lot of energy, but I feel that by eight, nine o'clock, when she's ready for them they don't have the concentration.

This year is the most I'm going. Why? My daughter called me [and said] my grandson was having a difficult time adjusting to fifth grade. He had hours of homework. My son-in-law is marvelous with electric trains, but he doesn't always have the patience for language and reading that I'm proficient in.

I was afraid it might be too intensive. It might cause an alienation between me and my grandson such as the Wicked Witch of the North was coming this afternoon to work with him. I agreed to try it and it worked phenomenally well. We've developed a real warm, loving relationship and he looks forward to me being there. If I'm not, he wants to know how come?

I try to give them independence, but I'm there at least three days a week from after school to 5:30. He could have two hours of homework, and the younger boy becomes jealous and he calls on me too.

I really enjoy it! I love knowing what they're doing. I [went] to the school and the teacher asked me to help *her* [because] I was familiar with the new techniques of reading and cooperative learning. I feel so lucky. I help them, then I go home to make dinner for my husband.

I'm also there to give my daughter and son-in-law a break because they're very conscientious parents. They would gladly have gotten a tutor, they can well afford it. But I love [being] with the boys and he's showing a lot of progress. I even taught poetry in their early grades, first and second. But by third grade, I thought I shouldn't be in their classroom, sometimes they'd call me grandma. This year I made it a point to [ask] my grandson if he was uncomfortable. And he said, 'No, it's great!'

When my daughter goes on vacation, I stay there. This year she went to Hong Kong and the Orient for two weeks on business, and I stayed. The nanny was there, [but] she does the housekeeping. I work with the children. I drive them to activities. When they were taking tennis lesson, I'd pick them up at school and take them there and drive them home. They gave me their soccer and basketball schedules and we'd go. It's a support they want. And on their school vacations, my husband and I try to take them someplace special. A museum. The planetarium.

[With an adult daughter], there's a fine line you have to walk. I don't want to tell her what to do. But if a child has a temperature and I [tell her] he should stay home an extra day, she says, 'Thanks' and she sends them to school anyway. She is the parent and I am the grandmother. The only time we get into an argument is if a child has a strep throat and she sends him to school in two days and takes him skiing. That, to me, is not the correct thing to do, but I have to let it go. My grandson had a sore throat and they never took him to the doctor, and a week later he had strep. I didn't say it, but I thought, *See?*

Discipline? Tension? We're extremely careful. But I don't think the children eat properly. I've said my piece. The nanny gives them treats before dinner and I think that's why they're not eating. It finally got to me and I told my daughter. They don't eat green vegetables or take vitamins, and I've mentioned [other] things. But I'm not there [all the time]. I held my tongue. I really *do* hold my tongue. I'm in the house a lot, which sometimes is not good [because] you see things.

[For example], too much television. Now they're into computer games. I think the parents indulge them too much. They get them more things than they need. The community they live in is an extremely competitive environment, very upscale. It's pretty much millionaire row. Parents are college educated and the children are competitive in fifth grade. If a child can't keep up, well…It's a public school, very highly rated, and I can see where [if] a child was a little slow and felt it, he'd be better off in another environment.

Why am I there? To give them an extra edge. I don't go to PTA meetings, no. But I got to know the parents when I went to the tennis courts and I could hear what's going on. How the kids were overly programmed and the *parents* [are] so competitive.

How are my grandchildren indulged? One house on the block—my grandson says it looks like a castle and he thinks this is how people live. The child's frame of reference is really very different than a lot of other children. They have a money allowance and they have no clue. They put it in the drawer and they have no value of it. They don't want to spend it. If they go [out] with me, they expect me to buy it, and I say, 'Okay, if you giver me half.' I tell the kids how I walked to school and took two busses, and they have no idea, no idea what it's like. They know their parents will buy them everything, so why should they spend their money? They don't have to save it. They're not doing what I think they should do.

Oh, they don't brag *look at my sneakers*, no, because everyone else has the same [expensive] sneakers. The older boy needed a sports jacket for the school concert. He plays the clarinet. His father takes him to a private teacher and the younger boy gets piano lessons. I figured I could [take him] to Daffy's and buy [the jacket] for $50. My daughter went to Bloomingdale's. She bought three and [let him] pick one, and she brought it to the tailor. The children have pretty much what they want. With her, time is more important than money. So she'll indulge them.

The parties they [attend] are extremely lavish. Pool parties. A private lifeguard [is hired]. A miniature golf course [is] set up. My grandson last year was picked up in a limo. That's the arena. A lot of money.

Sometimes I'm not too happy to feel obligated to be there. In the winter it's dark when I leave. The roads are curvy and icy. But I feel it's a commitment. I love the fact that I'm needed. I'm proud of my daughter. [But] I would like to see her not work so hard, work less hours per week. She doesn't have time for herself between her children, and her husband, and her job.

Her husband is a very nice man and they have a good marriage, and I'd hate to see any friction caused by the children because they can't get to help them. I'm reducing their stress load, I hope so. And I love working with the children. I'm not raising them. **I do it to enrich them. And they're enriching me.**

Discipline? If I say, 'I'm going to speak to mommy about this,' there's never a problem. It's worked out well. I feel a joy in helping the family.

Very often I *do* get tired. I lead a very busy life myself. I take an art course in New York, and they understand I'm not available to get home until three. It's a very long day for me. If someone is sick, I'm there during the day, and I hope I don't get sick [myself.] When they're away, I'll stay at the house. The nanny is a lovely woman, but she doesn't drive, and she doesn't have professional skills.

To become so dependent on having your grandchildren around— that's dangerous. I think I'd miss them. You feel left out if they don't need you anymore, or if the parents take over. I don't want to [feel dependent.]

Next year, my grandson is going to Middle School. It's a big adjustment. He's young for his age. If I'm well, I'll try to be there for him.

My husband will be retiring and he is going into my son-in-law's business. So my daughter and her family, we're very entwined. My son and his son? Oh, I miss them. They live in London.

I'm very careful. I don't want to get into my daughter's personal life. I resist it. My daughter appreciates me. I know she does. I never go there unless she knows I'm coming. I don't go and ring the bell.

Am I making my daughter's life possible? Comfortable? I hope so. I think so. It's a great pleasure. I see [other] women returning to this extended family concept.

You have to be very careful when you're that close. For example, sometimes I'll call her at night and she can't talk to me, she's too busy. So I'll feel resentful. The time I talk to her the most, believe it or not, is when she's in the car coming home from work and she has a half hour on the car phone. I can't call her [at home] until after ten at night. She's tired. That's the only time I get annoyed. And my head tells me I'm wrong. She needs time for herself.

A good tip for grandparents is to discipline yourself. And when you're at their house with the children, you're *not* the mother, you're the grandmother. Remember that!"

BETTY is like many grandparents today. She's proud of her child's financial success, but she's concerned that her grandkids are handed too many things and they're likely to face hard knocks in the real world. If grandparents are "depression babies," they are astonished by the excess and coddling of their grandkids.

Betty has a point. Privileged kids, handed a lifestyle of computers, cell phones, and credit cards, may wind up feeling conflicted. With dual-career parents working long hours, which is the norm today, some parents feel guilty and, to make up for it, they give their kids too much. You see these families traveling the highways in luxury minivans equipped with TV, Discman, and Nintendo. The *New York Times* (November 21, 2003) reports that on long car trips, "the back seat is becoming a rolling multiplex with the help of video gear from VCR's to satellite TV systems." To Betty, all of this is excess.

SMART TIPS FROM BETTY

If you plan to participate in your grandkids' school and talk to their teachers, ask them first if they're comfortable with this.

Don't tell your adult daughter or son how to raise their children. They are the parents, you are the grandparent.

Best to let some things go by, like arguments about food and children's illnesses.

Discipline yourself. Hold your tongue. Don't criticize the parent's attitudes and values.

Enrich your grandkids' cultural life. Take them to museums and planetariums.

Help them with homework if you can. Try to give them an edge toward success.

Don't overindulge your grandchildren. Don't buy them whatever they ask for.

Teach them to save money and to spend wisely.

Sometimes it's okay *not* to feel happy as a grandparent. Sometimes grandparenting feels like an obligation.

It's okay to feel tired and to say you're unavailable.

It's dangerous to become too entwined and too dependent on having grandkids around.

Avoid getting into your child's personal life. Don't drop in to see your
    grandkids.

When your child is too busy or too tired to talk on the phone, resist
    resentment.

Respect your child's job. Working parents need time for themselves.

In the next chapter, you will meet **SARAH,** a grandmother of sev-
enty-five, who took her infant grandson into her home twenty years
ago. And she's still raising him. Pool parties with limos? They're tab-
loid headlines to her. She glances at them on the check-out line at the
Grand Union as she counts out her double coupons.

4

SARAH

✦

My Daughter Died

It's nine a.m. on a bright May morning when I meet Sarah at the diner she has selected not far from her home.

"I'd be happy for you to come to the house, but my grandson might be home," she told me on the phone. "And well…some things I don't want him to hear."

She approaches me at the Formica booth, smiling. She has short, gray hair, no makeup, and only a swipe of lipstick. She's wearing a polyester navy suit, hem to her knees, low heel pumps, and a crisp, white blouse with lace trim, buttoned to the neck. On her left lapel is a gold pin, the G clef musicians recognize, a fitting selection for a church organist and choir director.

Sarah's eyes are weary. In a calm voice, she explains that it's been a tough year.

"My dear husband has gone through three surgical operations." A long sigh. "But he's looking better," she adds. "Considering he had knee replacement surgery, eye surgery, and now, just a week ago, he had a her-nia operation. He's eighty-three. The doctor says he's coming along. I'm very thankful, very thankful."

I ask about her own health.

"Me?" She puts on a brave face. "I have hypertension, high blood pressure, dangerously high, but I'm on medication. I have glaucoma and bladder problems. I just feel a little stressed out right now. But I

23

know each day I'll come back to where I was. See my husband is retired, but I'm still working."

SARAH, 75, is a grandmother raising her grandson. Eric is twenty now, a high school graduate working full time in the deli department of a large supermarket. It was a long, hard road. Sarah and her husband took him into their home when he was only three months old. Her eyes fill up as she tells the story.

"My daughter had been quite ill with diabetes. She tried to take care of him here in our home. Then she went into her own apartment. She would do her best, and we would keep a daily watch to see everything was all right.

Until one night, I kept calling and calling till 12:30, getting no answer, and I said to my husband, 'We have to go to New York and see what's going on.' That's where she lived, in the city. And we found her on the floor. In a coma.

So we brought the baby home and we had him full time. She'd take him for an overnight to have a union with her son, but physically she was not able. Her eyesight was getting very bad. She was legally blind.

And the father—they weren't married—he never wanted this child. He told her unless she got rid of it, he would leave her. Which he did. He abandoned her and never gave one cent of support for the child. So he was raised totally by me and my husband. We were 55 and 63, turned back thirty years. And suddenly, we're in full charge.

It was difficult. Not only [raising] the child, but a child not wanted. With that atmosphere in the background, it didn't have the full joy of a newborn. Plus the mother is very ill. Not only from the diabetes, but from the rejection of this man whom I assumed she loved. As an outsider looking in, and thinking of my daughter only, I thought he was a very cruel man. But it was her decision, not mine.

We had to hire someone to take care of the infant because my husband was still working full time and I had to go to Boston and stay there with her when she had her eye operations or she would be totally blind.

How did I cope with it all? Mentally? Emotionally?

I guess I'm the type of person when I'm put to the test, I know it's from God alone. So I get that extra strength to just keep going. I knew there was only one thing I had to do. Save my daughter's sight! And the only way was through the operations in Boston. I had to keep my mind on getting it done. She was thirty, my only child.

I was very concerned for the little one. But my husband's job enabled him to stop home to see everything was okay. He worked in the neighborhood for the water department, so he could pop in and check. Which he did. And we called each other every night. It was very stressful. But when I'm under stress, that's when I seem to have the strength. When things straighten out, that's when I collapse.

When little Eric was born, he was only four pounds, and they put him in an incubator for the first twelve hours. We didn't expect him to live. It was hard for the little one to come into this world. So small, and without a father, and with a very sick mother. With her [poor health], she had to have a caesarian.

I was working at the Hammond Music Center on Route 46 and I was giving organ and piano lessons there full time. And thank God I had the job to cover the expenses in raising the baby and the medical expenses for our daughter. [But then] the place closed up over night. It became very, very difficult when I lost my job. Eric was four. My daughter couldn't work. Just my husband working, supporting us, and my daughter and the boy.

We could have gone on welfare. In my own life, way back, we were always very, very poor. But as poor as we were, my Dad never asked for assistance. At one point, he held three jobs to keep us going. So it was inbred in me that you don't go asking for a hand out. I was always taught you work for what you get. At that time I was [also] working Sundays at the First Presbyterian Church. Not much money, but it was getting food on the table, and we had health insurance through my husband's job. My daughter's disability [payments] helped a little.

So I took on more at the church. I became the Choir Director. I was responsible for training the singers and giving performances at services. A busy job. Time consuming. I was also giving private piano lessons, driving some distance to people's homes. I was busy every day, every day. My husband retired at 65 with a [small] pension. At this point I was the sole source of income other than social security.

My daughter died at forty.

I can put it in a nutshell. Nobody knows the feeling of losing a child until they lose one. It's hard to put into words. I often feel this way: part of my body just died when I lost her. [Her eyes fill up and she dabs at them with a tissue.]

My daughter had married, and she had two more children. So now, they're growing up without a mother. My son-in-law is taking excellent care of them. When they were younger, we used to see a lot of them, but they have friends and they live in Manhattan. Eric sees his half-brother and half-sister and he's very good with them. The boy is now 14 and the girl is 12. When they come out here, they do video things with Eric and they spend time together. So I have three grandchildren from my daughter.

She died when Eric was nine. It was December of 1989. Her baby girl was a year-and-half and her little boy was going to be four. It was very difficult. **What I kept foremost in my mind was that my daughter was the mother. If she had certain wishes about how Eric should be raised, I put that uppermost. It was *her* child.**

One of her requests was Eric should go to Catholic School rather than public school. Public school would have been easier, being nearer our home and easier financially, [but] we did it. But in sixth grade, we had to stop because the tuition was getting higher, they wanted $1700 and another $100 for uniforms. You can stretch it just so far.

Before leaving Catholic School, [there] was an awful experience for Eric. One day out of the clear blue sky, he said to me, 'Nana, why didn't my father want me?' He felt rejected. He wanted to know what he had done wrong. I said, 'Eric, you've done nothing wrong. Your father just did not want children. It was not an Eric he didn't want. You want the truth? *That* is the truth.'

[We didn't know it then,] but his father ultimately married and had another family. *But we didn't know this.* After my daughter died in 1989, I was warned that I better find Eric's biological father because he could come and take Eric away. If Eric ever went to the hospital, who's going to sign? It should be the parent, not the grandparent. So we hired a private investigator. All I had was the father's social security number. At a cost of $200 a day, we got all the information we needed in fourteen days. How the father had a heart attack and had died in Pennsylvania in 1986.

So our Eric was an orphan, and now I had a *right* to be his legal guardian. We couldn't adopt. Because of our ages, they wouldn't allow us. So the death of his father actually turned our to be a stroke of luck. I said, 'They'll never take Eric away, they'll have to take him over my dead body.'

And the boy was glad to get out of Catholic school. It was just too much religion. He was a boy whose little mind was not geared to that. He had the influence of a Christian home, yes, but nothing was ever forced on him, you *can't* do this, you *can't* do that. We weren't Catholic. My daughter became Catholic for Eric's father, for him.

And Eric had a very unfortunate experience with one of the Catholic teachers. He was not a well child, he had a lot of allergies. And he was home ill a lot. The teacher came to visit. She brought a little something from the class, it put a smile on his face. And then she said, *with Eric sitting right there in a chair in front of us*, 'You ought to have Eric tested psychologically.' Right in front of Eric. As soon as she went out the door, he said, 'Nana, she thinks I'm crazy.'

It was devastating. What we went through at that time, nobody knows. I went to the principal and I said, 'We have to get out of here. Eric is not crazy and for the child to come out with that…' They said the teacher was upset because she was getting divorced, and I said, 'You don't carry your problems into your work, you leave them at home.'

For two or three days he wouldn't get out of bed. I just talked to him. I talked to him, and I talked to him. 'You're not crazy, you're not.' It was breaking my heart. I didn't want him to see it. I was trying to make it a nice conversation and get to the core. 'You are not crazy. You are fine.' I said, 'If you believe in God, just ask Him to help you and He will help you to forget this. I know you are *not* crazy. You have to forget this and put it behind you.'

This was sixth grade. He went into seventh grade in *public* school. It was like a rose opening up. I could see the transformation, we were so thankful. He said the kids were friendly. For a while, he was very bitter on life. He's an introvert. And as a teenager, to think he had no parents at all, well…

Of the two of us, I was more strict than my husband. At times I was greatly rejected by Eric. He would say, 'Other [kids] do this and that.' And I'd say, 'Whatever their parents allow, that's in their household, not in this one. The one thing I do want is respect.' I told him this. 'On a few occasions you have shown a little disrespect, namely to your grandmother. Don't ever let it happen again. While you're under my roof, it's the one thing I demand. Other things we'll negotiate. But I demand respect from you. Learn to have it for yourself first. And you'll have it for us.'

One incident. When he came home, and he had been drinking and was in sad shape. It was after midnight. I thought he should be home or just call me, that's all I ask. When he came in, I said, 'Eric, I want a nice little talk with you. For your own sake, I'm asking you, don't follow this path, don't follow this path of drinking. Your father was more drunk than he was sober and that's why he was so mean to your mother. The drinking problem grew, and he couldn't do without it. I'm making it very clear. I have no tolerance with a drunk. I will not put up with a drunken person.'

He said, 'You can't tell me what to do, you're not my mother.'

Then I said, 'You're absolutely right, I'm not your mother. But if it wasn't for us, stop to think where you would be. If there's anything you owe us, it's to listen. And when you're of age, do whatever you want. But until that time, you owe it to us to follow our wishes.'

Did I feel resentful, angry? Oh, yeah. And even before that, way back, when my daughter became totally blind, and I had to do everything for her and care for her baby. He only slept an hour-and-a-half at a time. I asked God to forgive me, carrying that grudge and the guilt feelings. But it did hit me then, too.

Since I've come to know the Lord, I go to Him at times and He's promised that he will help us. He'll give us strength to go through these periods and I know He's not going to forsake us. I am a person of strong faith and so is my husband. I feel the values I got and it's my obligation to give this to my grandson. As poor as we were, we had love for each other. It carried us through many, many a tight situation.

We gave Eric chores. Taking out the garbage. Getting his homework done. I explained his situation to the school and they put him in Special Education. It was the greatest thing, they were opening the door up that had been closed. In high school, they did it right up to the time he graduated. One period was with an instructor. She helped him do his homework, showed him how to correlate everything, and how to study for a test. And through it, he got more confidence. And his friend got him a job part-time in the supermarket even before he graduated. [We were] happy to see how everything was turning out.

What about disciplining him as a teenager? If it was dangerous to do, I would just block it. But other than that, I would try to sit down with him and say, 'Look at it this way, look at it the other way. Which is going to be better for you?' I'd say, 'I made plenty of mistakes, but I always listened to my parents. You've got to think it through and choose.'

Thank God he never got in contact with drugs, he was never involved. Sex? Not that I know of. Due to our ages, foremost in my mind was to prepare him [for] when he's alone. My daughter's husband has total care of our other two [grandchildren]. I don't know if he'd take over.

In my will, Eric gets half of everything. The other half is divided [between] the two other grandkids. My son-in-law cannot touch the money, and my lawyer is the Executrix. Any money that's given out has to go through her. When Eric turns 21, he deals with her himself. We have the mortgage paid.

The victories? Well…his high school diploma! And now he's full time at the supermarket with medical benefits. And he's saving for a car. He gives us a little something each week which we're thankful for. But other than that, he covers all his own expenses. We've made it clear he has to pay his own bills. I haven't taught any private pupils since last year. Just the church job. The first check Eric brought home, he handed it to us and said, 'For all that you've done for me, I want you to have this.' I tell you, I'll never, never forget that!

It's taken timeless hours. My whole focus was on my daughter and [raising] this baby. But it's all paid off in wonderful dividends. We're still trying to prepare this boy for his life after ours ceases. Twenty is a lot different from 75 and 83. And that he'll think clearly and make wise decisions and [it will] come back to his memory to say *Is this right or wrong?* If we can accomplish that, then I feel we have done our part as grandparents.

When I get depressed, I just keep very busy. During the night I have cleaned many a drawer out at three in the morning, until I got so tired I went back to bed and fell asleep. Anything my husband and I disagreed on we never spoke about in front of Eric. I stayed calm. Any crisis in life, I've come to know the Lord and He has promised to help me in every situation. That's where the calmness takes over. I talk to God. 'I don't know what to do, and if you don't help me, I don't know…'

There's been moments. Crying spells, but never hysteria. I just learned through all of this that I had to be calm and try to help [my daughter] and try to guide Eric and watch my husband also. If I'm going to become hysterical, everything's going to pot. One time I threw Eric into the bed. Now he's six foot one, taller than I am.

Due to our financial status, I had to work most of the time. So I wasn't able to do many things with him. But we watch TV. Baseball mostly. Keeping the communication channels open at all times is important. You want to be a friend, not just a grandparent. And yes, correct him. But do it with sincere love.

I'm proud of Eric. I gave him values. I see parents who give their kids everything, but they have no goals. When he said, 'Other kids don't have to pay anything at home, why do I have to pay?' I said, 'We're not in that category. You'll never regret it. I worked for $19 a week and gave my check, minus the bus fare, to my mother.'

I'm so proud of this boy. Thank my dear God, he's in good health. He's a hard worker. He's been there two years and has not missed one day of work. He's a good boy. We're very proud of him."

SMART TIPS FROM SARAH

Older grandparents raising a grandchild have to pay attention to their own medical problems.

If your child is too ill to raise a child, take on that job. You will find the extra strength to keep going.

When your bills pile up and you lose your job, don't go asking for a handout. Work harder.

If your child dies, keep foremost in your mind what *her* wishes were about how to raise your grandchild.

When the father has abandoned the family, you have to deal with your grandchild's feelings of blame and rejection.

If your grandchild is an orphan, you have the additional burden of his grief and fears.

Consult a lawyer and investigate your legal options for guardianship.

Be a friend, not just a grandparent.

Correct. But do it with sincere love.

Be strict. Do not accept disrespect. Negotiate other things.

If your teenage grandchild is drinking, explain the dangers of following that path. Be firm. Do not put up with it.

You may have crying spells, but don't get hysterical. Stay calm in a crisis.

If your grandchild defies you and says, "You're not my mother, I don't have to listen to you," insist he must follow your rules until he is of age.

You are bound to feel *resentful* at times. And you are going to feel *guilty* about this.

It is your obligation to give your grandchildren goals and values.

Ask your teenage grandchild to do chores around the house.

Go to your grandchild's school and share information about his special situation.

Ask for extra help and see that your grandchild gets it.

Encourage your teenage grandchild to get a part-time job. It teaches confidence.

Be proud of your grandchild's accomplishments.

Make it clear that a grandchild who has a full time job must pay his own bills.

If your grandchild does something dangerous, use persuasion and explain calmly what the choices are.

Older grandparents raising a grandchild should prepare for their death and make plans for when their grandchild is alone.

Consult a lawyer and make a will.

Enjoy the victories of raising a grandchild to adulthood. It's an accomplishment.

Raising a grandchild pays off in wonderful dividends.

5

LIN

✦

I Became Their Nanny

So far you've heard *three grandmothers* tell their stories and offer coping methods from their experiences. You probably noticed that they have different points of view, and sometimes they don't agree. Their **SMART TIPS** reflect their own personal life and their own personal style of grandparenting. And that's fine. What works for one family may not work for another.

ALICE, for example, is the boss in her family. She owns the home the three generations live in. So when she thinks her daughter or her grandson is making a mistake, all she has to do is give them the *look*. That's the warning, and it works.

BETTY, on the other hand, is very careful about not stepping on her daughter's toes. When she visits her daughter's home and sees something she doesn't like, she holds her tongue. Her daughter has the final word because she is the parent.

SARAH was forced into the role of parent to her infant grandson. She was bewildered and exhausted. This is tough enough when you're in your fifties. But when you're in your seventies, facing money problems and heath problems, the burden can feel pretty heavy.

Okay, *three different grandmothers.*

Different situations. Different attitudes. Different lives.

Now it's time to meet a grandfather. Only this one is not your typical American grandpa who takes his grandkids to baseball games and buys them hot dogs. It's a story about how one grandfather, who was a businessman living half-way around the world, left his country and came to the United States to become the nanny to his two little granddaughters. You don't have to be from Taiwan to relate to what this grandfather has to say.

LIN, 67, is Chinese. He lives with his daughter, her husband, and their two little girls, 9 and 8. Their home is a spacious contemporary in a suburban town of excellent schools, beautiful homes, and high taxes. They are a three generation Chinese family. Lin immigrated from Taiwan when his grandchildren were barely one and two.

Lin's daughter, 40, is running late and won't be home from work until 8:30. She commutes to New York daily. So her husband graciously welcomes me into their living room and says he will act as translator for his father-in-law, whose English is limited. When Lin's daughter arrives, she will take over.

Lin is a small, smiling man. We shake hands and take seats beside each other with the tape recorder on the coffee table. I admire the ebony baby grand piano and ask, "Who plays?" Lin answers proudly. "Both girls play, and the-nine-year old is studying flute."

I ask Lin what are his tasks in his daughter's home? And we begin. His son-in-law helps him find the right words in English when Lin gets stuck.

"My tasks? I take my grandchildren to school every day. I drive them there and drive them home. That's my job. Also piano lessons and gymnastics, and I drive them to SCORE. That's a computer assisted learning center because their parents have no time.

While they are in school, I go to play golf. When I'm free, I go to a health club to swim in the pool. I get home in time to take them to their activities. Usually I get them home, have snack with them, and in thirty minutes we go to next activity.

Is there a language problem? No. Both children understand and speak Taiwanese and Mandarin perfectly, and I make sure they understand. I am Christian, but my daughter and her family are not Christian.

Why do I want to do this? What is my motivation?

I do this because my grandchildren are the most precious in my life. I am watching them grow up.

The parents work and I want to help out. I want to enjoy my grandchildren. We do things together. I see that they study hard and they get good grades in school. I am retired, so I have the time to do this.

Before I retired, I owned a factory that produced electronic equipment in Taiwan. I am here since 1992. My grandchildren were maybe one and two, babies. I wanted to help the family out. My daughter and son-in-law work long hours. Begin 6 a.m. and end 8:30 p.m. like today.

What happened is the parents had great difficulty finding nannies. That was the reason I came from Taiwan. They could not find nanny to take care of babies, *two* babies at the same time. You can't trust nannies. No, no. My wife came over to help too. Now she goes back and forth. We argue a lot about modern things. My wife is here six months, and she returns to Taiwan six months of the year. When we disagree, we speak in Japanese so the children don't understand. [He laughs.]

The parents have very demanding jobs. You see it's 8:30 and my daughter, she hasn't even eaten her dinner. And her husband works long hours. He leaves the house at six, and is in his office at eight. He used to commute 75 minutes each way, but not now. So I became the nanny they could trust.

What values do I want to give my grandchildren?

First of all, I want them to know themselves. How to take care of their own bodies and their health. They need to learn this. *Second,* they need to learn how to save money. How to value money. I show them you can't waste money and it's not easy to make money. It's difficult."

[Lin's daughter arrives home. We greet each other, and she slips quietly onto the sofa next to her husband, not to intrude. Her girls come rushing in, tumbling all over their mother, giggling, charming, and not a bit shy. But when their parents shush them, they are obedient and respectful. "Grandpa is speaking. Quiet." Lin continues.]

"I want them to understand what they have to start looking for. What do they want to do in the future? They need to start considering their goals. Basically, I show them by example. If they see a doctor, I explain to them what it takes to become a doctor. They see their parents, and I explain what it takes to be a computer consultant. [To reach] the position is a long road. To achieve the results is hard work. And it doesn't come easy.

Are there values in our culture that I want my granddaughters to have?

Yes, yes. The basic value that is foremost in Chinese culture is the concept of family. *That they obey the elders.* They must get along with siblings. They may not accept this completely, but that's where the parents come in, to help out and explain, to let them understand [rather than] force them. Parents must say, 'You can't be rude to your grandparents.' That's definitely a no-no. If they wanted to watch a TV show and I thought it inappropriate, they would never say, 'No. You're not my parent.' Never, never. No. They know grandpa is the boss.

What happens when there's a conflict between generations? The parents want it one way and the kids want it another way. Well, the grandchildren want what they see in American school. Then the parents say, 'We are Chinese. We do it the Chinese way at home.' The parents enforce these values even if it contradicts what they see in school. Which is—yes I can say it—*spoiled brats,* at times. In this house, we are Chinese and that's how we do it.

Do I get instructions from the parents? Not specifically, not every day. We basically understand what needs to be done. The grandchildren know the rules, and if there's any conflict, if the kids break the rules, I let the parents know if they're not listening to me and [if their] behavior is good or bad. Yes, I let them know.

The kids are not perfect. The nine-year-old wanted her ears pieced. I said, 'No, no, no.' They need to follow what we tell them, and they know what the punishment is. They don't have TV for the weekend. The parents reinforce that *the grandparents are the boss*. The parents reinforce what grandpa says.

The children like their school and their teachers. But they also go to a Chinese school. About 12 to 15 in a class. Enrollment about 185 to190 students. We are the only Cantonese language school in the area, so people who want to learn Cantonese all come to us from other counties. The school has two libraries: Mandarin and Cantonese. Parents want their children to learn to write and to know more about religion and history.

What are the most fun things we do together? Rollerblading? Oh, no, no, no. The children don't like to go fishing, so I don't take them. Only once. We caught crabs at a bay. I gave them away. And the girls sprayed air freshener, they used up half a can, they said it smelled disgusting.

I cook for them, yes. Sometimes they say it's good and sometimes it's in the middle. Their favorite dish is Chinese cabbage with butter and milk and salt. We had it for dinner today. They love it.

The girls have very busy schedules and I'm their driver. Sometimes I bring their cousins here. It makes them happy and they play together. They have very demanding lives. They go to gymnastics. They play piano and one plays flute. They take private lessons with American teacher and they give recitals. Almost five years. One girl began lessons on the piano at four years old. She practices 45 minutes a day and the younger one 20 minutes a day.

Do Chinese families worry about drugs and teenage pregnancy and the American culture of giving too much? When the child does something well, we encourage them with a reward system. [They get] a dollar from the parents. Me? I give them a candy. If they get 100 at SCORE, the private computer center, I reward them for good spelling. I don't know the computer and grandma doesn't either. As reward, my daughter takes them shopping to the mall.

No allowances. But the Red Envelope at Chinese New Year, yes. It varies, it goes by the lunar year. After dinner, in January, we give the children the Red Envelope. Twenty dollars! The girls don't spend it, they collect it, they keep it. They save it in the bank for their college education.

Both parents have college education. My son-in-law has Masters in Computer Science and MBA. My daughter has Masters in Library and Information Sciences on the computer. She works in New York and commutes every day. She says it would be impossible to manage without me. She comes home late from Manhattan. She couldn't do this without me.

She says, 'Without my father here with the children, I could not do this.' She goes to New York with peace of mind. That is the biggest. She doesn't have to worry about anything happening at home. It's beyond description. It works. She says I'm very competent. She says I'm conscientious. And very considerate. For example, I have dinner waiting for them when they get home from work.

Basically, I work around their schedule. I'm very active in my church. But if she says, 'Daddy, I can't be home at a certain time,' I say, 'Don't worry, I'll be there.' Absolutely. She relies on me entirely. My judgments. My schedule. My competence.

What will happen ten, twenty years from now? When I'm 77, 87, 97? When I'm not so competent? Then it will be *their* turn to take care of me. My daughter's turn. Will she do a good job? Yes, yes!

[The nine-year-old serves me a glass of hot water.]

There is not much conflict with us. Some people have big emphasis on family values and some have less. The biggest problem with the grandchildren is they say, 'Why do we have to learn Chinese? Why do we have to go to Chinese School?' We say, 'You are Chinese children. Look at the Jewish [people.] They have to learn Hebrew and go to Hebrew School two, three times a week.'

Will the girls be tempted when they go to college? My daughter is not concerned at this point because the grandchildren have presented themselves to be *disciplined*. They know what's right and wrong in most part. If they do something and my daughter [is] upset with their behavior, she typically will tell them. I don't discipline them. But I will tell my daughter what's going on and why grandpa [was] upset with their behavior, and then she will explain to them.

What Chinese values do we want to pass on? Family values. Being ethical. To work hard. My wife and I taught our daughter to work hard. But she says, 'It's more important to work smart.' Work *hard*, for the grandchildren, is to study and learn a lot. But work *smart* is to work more efficiently. I don't show them how to work smart, my daughter does.

That's the most difference between the generations, between my daughter and me. She gives them leisure to watch TV. But we feel, my wife and me, they must always study hard. That's the conflict between our generations. We think they spoil the kids too much. They buy them things. Me? I give them a hug and a kiss. A candy.

This is a prosperous town and some kids get cars when they graduate high school. My daughter teaches them if they put ten dollars away in the bank, she will put in another ten dollars, matching funds, as a reward. It teaches them to save. It works!

We have relatives in the area nearby. The grandchildren have aunts and uncles and cousins. Are they jealous [because] I am in my daughter's home? No. Sometimes I go there to visit the three-year-old grandson. I help my other daughter too. I make myself available. There is no such thing as jealousy between sisters and brothers. I have no regrets about immigrating.

My daughter hopes as the grandchildren get older, she will be less dependent on me. Right now my schedule is tied to my grandchildren's schedule. And she says it's not fair to me. She hopes in the future I can enjoy life more. She feels a little guilty.

But I'm out on the golf course for hours. And on weekends I go fishing. And I go to church every Sunday."

You probably noticed that **LIN** echoes some of **BETTY'S** attitudes. Both are concerned about spoiling grandkids by giving them too much. **LIN'S** granddaughters go to Chinese school to study Cantonese, Chinese history, and religion. **BETTY'S** grandsons go to Hebrew school to study Jewish history, Hebrew, and Torah. *Family, education, and hard work* are strongly stressed in both homes.

SMART TIPS FROM LIN

Help your grandchildren to examine their goals.

Explain the hard work it takes to achieve a worthwhile position.

Show them how to take care of their health and their bodies.

Teach them how to save money and how difficult it is to make money.

Set up matching funds. If they put $10 in the bank, add another $10.

If you help raise your grandchildren, their parents can go to work with peace of mind.

Honor the concept of family. Children must be taught to get along with their siblings.

Children must obey their elders. This is fundamental to family life.

Grandchildren must show respect to grandparents, rudeness is not tolerated.

Grandchildren can not disobey grandparents. We are the boss.

Let the grandchildren know the rules and what the punishments are.

Teach grandchildren their cultural heritage so they know their history, religion, and native language.

Cook your grandchildren their favorite foods.

Encourage your grandchildren to take music lessons, gymnastics, and computer training.

Help them to save for their college education.

Drive your grandchildren to their activities to take the stress off their parents.

Do things for yourself. Set aside time to enjoy golf or fishing.

Show the parents that you are reliable and competent, and your judgments about raising grandchildren are sound.

Do your grandparenting well and one day it will be your child's turn to take care of you.

Teach grandchildren discipline early. Later, they will be prepared when temptations arise.

Don't spoil your grandchildren. Give them hugs and kisses and modest rewards.

Grandchildren are the most precious in your life. Watch them grow.

So far, all the grandparents you've met are grandparents to the children of their children. They are *related by blood*. It's easy to love your children's children. It feels natural to adore them. One has grandpa's chin and one has grandma's smile. You can even argue about who gave them their musical talent or athletic ability.

But what happens when your child becomes a stepparent to someone else's children? Suddenly you've got *step*-grandchildren. How do you deal with that? With about 50% of American marriages ending in divorce, and remarriage producing blended families, step-grandparents are now part of the American family.

In the next chapter you'll meet **JUDY,** a step-grandmother who tells us how she reacted to two angry step-grandchildren.

6

JUDY

✦

Two Step-grandchildren

JUDY stands tall, about five foot eight, and she is straight as an arrow. No cane, no hearing aid, not even a pair of eyeglasses on her nose. She moved to Florida thirteen years ago, but she returns to her native New Jersey frequently to visit her children, grandchildren, great-grandchildren and step-grandchildren, a huge extended family.

She is a widow on a fixed income, so I ask her how she can afford these trips.

"My kids send me tickets, how else?" She grins merrily, and opens her pocketbook. "Want to see their pictures?" For a few minutes she passes snapshots to me, explaining proudly who belongs to what family, and adding a little anecdote about each grandchild's accomplishments.

She is wearing black slacks and a raspberry sweater, with a colorful silk scarf tied around her neck. On this cold winter afternoon, the sky is starting to darken, but she is bright and energetic.

JUDY is 82, but she looks a decade younger. She is the mother of three daughters, grandmother of five grandchildren, and step-grandmother of two. She is also a great-grandmother of three. "I make frequent treks north so I can keep close to all of them. I stay with old friends."

She tells me she has just come from the beauty salon and pats her graying hair which is styled nicely around her cheerful face. She has light gray eyes and a square jaw. Make no mistake about her. She is a no-nonsense woman who speaks her mind.

"I graduated from Mt. Sinai School of Nursing. I was trained as a psychiatric nurse, and I worked my whole life. When my husband died, I was fifty-three, a widow with three daughters. I had to keep working and I threw myself into work. Why? I needed the money. But I also did a great deal of volunteer work for interracial and Jewish causes."

There is an intensity about this woman as she leans in to tell her story. "I took on two surly, difficult step-grandchildren. They were deeply disturbed over the divorce of their father, my son-in law. What a challenge."

This is a situation many step-grandparents are facing because the number of children raised by *stepparents* has increased dramatically. Shared custody has become a common arrangement when parents get divorced. So stepchildren are living part-time in different homes.

So far, *we have no statistics on step-grandparents.*

I asked Ethel Dunn, Executive Director of *Grandparents United For Children's Rights*, if she had any information on *step*-grandparents. This is an organization that has tons of information and is very active. (Look for it under Resources and Organizations in the back of this book.) She told me, "I wish I did. This is an issue that hasn't been researched enough."

Here's what Judy says about her experience as step-grandmother to her daughter Rachel's two stepchildren.

"What's the secret ingredient? **Love. Love is the secret ingredient**. My daughter had her hands full with her two stepchildren. When Mary was four and Ronald was three, they started spending summers with Rachel and her husband. It wasn't easy because they had gone through a very turbulent life with their mother, and she blamed the divorce on my daughter. She told her children their daddy left them to marry a Jewish girl and my daughter Rachel was the reason why he left his family in England to go to the United States. Not true!

But I felt so sorry for them. Their mother was born in India on a tea plantation. My son-in-law Edward was the manager of the plantation. Their mother became pregnant and Edward felt he had to marry her. He was a proper Englishman.

When he came to the United States on business, he met my daughter. He was getting divorced, and she was a single woman working as a translator. I was concerned. I said, 'Rachel, he's not Jewish, he's getting divorced, and he has two children. How many commandments have you broken?' And she said, 'Mom, you always taught us to judge the individual.'

Three years later they married and she became his executive secretary. His children lived with their mother in England, and the arrangement was they came to stay here for summer visitation. They were really messed up. Very vulnerable.

When my daughter told me they were going to live with her and her husband permanently, I asked her, 'How will you manage? What will you do?' They were seven and eight years old.

She said, 'Mom, Edward will be miserable if I don't take them.'

I knew I had to help her.

My daughter and her husband had two little girls of their own at that time. They were three years old and six months, and she was nursing the baby when she got the step-kids. I was very concerned. So I asked her, 'If it's too much, what will you do?' And she told me that she and her husband talked it over. 'If they endanger our marriage, the kids will have to go back to England. Edward and I agreed.'

I remember the little boy at the dinner table. Ronald would *not* eat chicken with his fingers. We did. I said, 'It's okay, honey, just pick it up and eat it.' But he couldn't. He was so proper, he couldn't do it. His sister Mary was the opposite. Angry. Troubled to this day. The boy was a cry baby, very namby-pamby, and the girl was angry, very angry.

Two troubled children. And my daughter was working very hard, long hours in her husband's business.

How did I treat them?

I never said a cross word to them because I knew I had to lean over backwards to get them to trust me. I had to be good and caring. I was trained as a psychiatric nurse, so I understood the dynamics of jealousy. I treated each child as an individual. Each child would get whatever they needed, would get theirs as they needed it.

I bought them very wonderful birthday presents. I wanted to make them feel special. When the little girl got difficult, I'd distract her. I'd do things with her, not blame her. I'd fix her doll's dress and I'd give her some grown up things to do with me. Like help me with the laundry. Or I'd ask her to help me with the cooking. We'd bake brownies together.

It was hard. Because she *hated* my daughter. She had a mother in England, so she hated her stepmother. She'd say to me, 'Your daughter! She has a maid, plays tennis, and is always out having a good time.' She was so full of anger and resentment. Once, as a gift, Rachel and her husband sent Mary back to England to see her mother who had an illegitimate child. And was she happy to come back to us!

I'd stay with them two, three weeks at a clip. When the parents went away, I'd keep their routines, take them to soccer and tutoring and ice skating. I had to drive on this highway which was not fun. I was their chauffer, their housekeeper, their cook, and their nanny. And we'd stop for a sweet treat at Carvel on the way home. I gave them *extra* care and consideration so they'd feel loved.

How did I manage it? How did I handle them? They were my step-grandchildren and their lives were disrupted. The least I could do was to be understanding. I had to be kinder to them because they needed it. It wasn't easy.

Sometimes when I saw the girl push my own grandchild, I had to hold back. I did not report it. Never. Never would I tattle to my daughter. I never got in the middle of it. I let my daughter do her discipline without my interference. I'd bite my tongue and swallow.

If one child said, 'She hit me,' and the other said, 'She hit me first,' I had them both do a chore. They had to learn to work out problems. I treated them like they were my own grandchildren, but I also gave them extra special care. Of course, I gave my own grandchildren their extra special care too. But I was careful to do it when [the others] weren't around. I guess I'm a sensitive soul.

I feel very lucky. It was hard work and a lot of pain and grief, but it paid off. The step-grandchildren had some counseling and that helped. But most important? Love. That's the secret ingredient."

SMART TIPS FROM JUDY

Recognize that taking on difficult step-grandchildren is a real challenge.

Step-grandchildren can be angry and miserable over their parents' divorce. Be sensitive to their situation.

Love is the secret ingredient.

Help your child to meet the demands of taking stepchildren into the home.

When step-grandchildren interact with the other grandchildren, there's bound to be fighting.

Step-grandchildren, who are from another culture, present a special challenge. Accept that their values are different from the rest of the family.

Lean over backwards to get them to trust you.

Treat each child as an individual. Give them what they need as they need it.

Make them feel special. Give them wonderful birthday presents. Pay attention to them.

When they are difficult, distract them. Don't blame them.

Do things together. Fix a doll's dress. Ask them to help with grown-up chores.

Accept that there will be jealousy, even hatred, among the grandchildren and step-grandchildren.

Anger and resentment are bound to occur when children move into a stepparent's home.

Keep their routine when you are in charge. Drive them to activities and cook for them.

Show your step-grandchildren extra care and consideration so they feel loved.

Be understanding and kinder because their lives have been disrupted and they need special attention.

When a step-grandchild fights with your own grandchild, hold back and don't tattle to the parents.

Teach your step-grandchildren to work out their problems.

When you give extra care to your grandchildren, do it when your step-grandchildren aren't around.

When you help your step-grandchildren, you are reducing stress in your child's marriage.

In the next chapter, you are going to meet **KEISHA**, a grandmother who was in and out of jail for many years. Today she is raising four grandchildren, holding down a job, and going to college.

7

KEISHA

✦

Drug Addict and Prostitute

This is a sad story, full of tragedy and pain. You will see how one grandmother, *against all odds,* triumphed over her own miserable circumstances and turned her life around. Then, just as she got on her feet, just as she was feeling good about herself, she had to step in and become the parent to four grandkids.

You remember Alice, who raised her grandson because her daughter was a young, unwed mother. And Sarah, who raised her grandson when her daughter fell ill and died. These stories are sad too. But Alice and Sarah each had a solid family life. That doesn't mean no problems. Everyone has problems. But Alice and Sarah had working husbands and jobs of their own, and they lived safely in homes they owned. With their strong family backgrounds, they brought support to the grandparenting crisis they faced.

Keisha's story is much more complicated because her own life was in despair. Then, just when she thought she had climbed out of a pit of terror and was back on track, *she had to take over raising four grandchildren.*

Keisha, 44, is a tall, light-skinned black woman, very slim, hair cropped short, a Halle Berry type, except for her metal eyeglasses. I pick her up at the department store where she works part-time, and we drive to a restaurant. She asks for a cup of tea before we give the order.

She bows her head and says Grace. It's the day after Thanksgiving, a big shopping day across America, and she's tired and hungry.

Keisha is raising four grandchildren. The girls are eight, six, and five, and the baby boy is two. The grandkids are the children of her unmarried daughter, 26, a drug addict who lives in Pennsylvania. Another grandchild is in foster care in Trenton. Keisha's husband of ten years is "disabled," but he minds the kids when she can't be home. She is also a part-time college student. These are her words.

"I was a drug addict. I was on everything. Heroine, cocaine, you name it. For 20, 25 years. I was a prostitute in Newark. I was born in Montclair and I went to school there. Got on drugs at 15. Back and forth to jail. The last time I was in jail, I was in a bad state because I had cocaine poisoning and I broke out with sores all over my body. I got *saved* in jail. The Lord saved me in jail.

The cocaine poisoning had affected my nervous system and my hair fell out. I had sores and they stank. I was sitting in jail cleaning sores, and I just felt so bad about the things I was doing. I laid on the bed crying, thinking how different my life should be and I started calling the name of the Lord. 'Jesus, help me, help me, help me.' All the sins I committed flashed before my face and I looked up through the bars. I could see a light. It illuminated the whole cell. At the end of the light was a cross.

On Sunday, I went to church and I got delivered. I got deliverance! Everybody was holding hands in a circle. We were praying. All of a sudden, something knocked me on the floor. A force. The Holy Spirit. I began to scream and kick and fight. The officers ran in, they thought I was having an asthma attack. The Reverend said, 'Just leave her alone.' I was fighting a demon, fighting to break free, it didn't want to leave. And when I got up off the floor, I felt so light. I felt happy. And I went back to my cell.

And the next Sunday, the guard said, 'You're going home.' God had opened the prison doors. Because I had 15 bench warrants that I was waiting to go to court on, and my bail was $3000. So I knew it was the Lord.

I came home [to where] I used to live on Prince Street. *I lived in a shooting gallery.* I was so scared to go back in there. [But] I went in and lived there until I got married. [Lived] in the same place I used to get high and run with prostitutes and just used the money for drugs.

In 1989, I got married and my daughter came to live with me. She was fifteen and she had her first [baby] at seventeen. She's [still] on drugs. Her second baby, they found drugs in her urine. DYFS called, they have to take them away. And that's how I got those two. She was unfit, the point was the drugs. So I had to take on her babies. *I didn't want to, I didn't want to, I really didn't.* Because I had just started college, and life was good. You know everything that I had missed is what I [was] doing.

When I got them home, I thought about what I did to her, [and] I said, 'Well, I think I owe her.' It was my responsibility to help my daughter and my grandchildren. How could I be so selfish [and say], 'No, I can't take them because I'm going to college and I'm working.' I remember how [bad] I made my daughter feel, sending her off when she was five. She cried and cried.

And [then] she's pregnant again. Well, with the first two, my husband said, 'You have to do it. These are your grandchildren.' He was working then for a security company. So here comes the third one and this baby is *really* addicted. She has all kinds of complications, [stayed] in the hospital a month. The father was doing drugs and so was my daughter. [This time] my husband didn't have to encourage me. It was just pitiful, with the tubes coming out of her. I started getting welfare. There was another baby, I can't even remember the little girl's name. Oh, it's a shame. She's in foster care.

I was going to school. I was trying to get a degree in Drug Treatment Counseling. It's taking me a long time. I need maybe twelve more credits. Four classes. The last semester I was there was the last available funds I could get for a two-year college [to] move on to a four-year college. I had started working at the Marriott at the airport. Housekeeping. It was summer and I took Summer I and Summer II, but I didn't complete those classes. It was too rough. With the kids and working, it was too rough. I withdrew from one of the classes, but the other three classes I forgot to withdraw, so the incompletes became F.

I got my transcript two weeks ago. I'm praying that God will open up some means for me to get some money. Now my daughter, she's [still] on drugs, along comes another baby and he's a boy. So that's why I took him. The only boy.

How do I manage with four? I've learned how to do much with little. When I worked at Sears, I got four coats for seventy bucks for the kids. Together with my husband, we have $1400 maybe. Rent $600, $650. My husband is disabled, I don't want to talk about it. He stays home. I'm working anywhere from 20 to 35 hours. I pay my bills. I have health insurance, Horizon Mercy, through the welfare when I don't work. Medications free. It covers me and the four kids. Not the husband, he gets Medicaid.

It's been hard. No one as a back-up. Not a neighbor or a friend. Everybody is too busy. *The Program for Parents* helps. They pay a portion of the childcare, maybe 70, 80% the state pays. And there's one through *Work First, New Jersey*. Without them, I couldn't do it. I'd have to stay home. You find the care and they pay for it. And that frees you to go to school [or] work. They wouldn't pay for my college though. A three credit course, it's about $1000.

But I go to school now though *Work First*. I go Tuesday and Thursday evenings for Medical Insurance Billing. I'll get a certificate. The first section was on medical terminology, the second part was computers in the office. The next section will be coding. The last one is patient billing. I love it, I love it!

I was [also] doing Dance Ministry in the church. I was a minister in training, so I took Effective Speech, English 109. I love it. Absolutely, absolutely. In March, I won't have a degree, I'll have a certificate. I could work in a insurance company, a hospital, yes, [with] some kind of benefits.

Two months ago, I received a scholarship application from Horizon Mercy. I just absolutely couldn't believe it. And I was saying, 'Lord, I got to get back to school.' But I don't have any money. I'm in default on a loan, so I'm not eligible for financial aid. I have to pay my loan off, $2650. I'm waiting, I'm waiting. I mailed [the application] in. I got a recommendation letter from one of my professors, the Director of the Drug Treatment. I took the class he taught, the Internship Class. I think I'm in the running. He explained to them in his letter that I ran out of funds and I only have four classes left to get my degree, four more courses to take.

My health? It's good. I mean some days are better than others. I just had a hysterectomy, they found cancerous cells in my uterus. I rely on God. I pray every day. [And] I started smoking again, that's why I don't preach.

My husband helps me out so much these days. I had it real hard with my husband. He was getting high and sometimes he would take the rent money so we would have to move. But he's a real blessing these days. He's more off than on. It's like we traded places. He does the cleaning, he does the laundry, he sends the kids to school, he's there when I get home. Now we're doing the grandparenting together. He complains some days, but he seems to be satisfied.

We don't go out much, we don't even go out to eat. But we like old movies, we like musicals. We watch Fred Astaire and Ginger Rogers. Oh, the kids love that. Mary Poppins. Chitty-Chitty-Bang-Bang. We rent videos and watch together. We let them pick. For Christmas I'm going to get them Nintendo, it's about a hundred bucks. I'll put it on layaway and then just pay like that. They like Barbie [and] baby dolls. They like playing games. Checkers. Trouble. We all play. We just got a computer. They teach us the necessity for computers in the office. You don't have to run to a file room or a file cabinet. And everyone can view the same information at the same time. I love it. Absolutely, I love it.

[What I'm lousy at is]…the other night we were cooking and my little granddaughter said, 'Grandma, Papa talk and you get the belt.' I'm not much of a talker these days. I've got zero tolerance for the nonsense. We have talked about being disobedient. 'You're not to do that, it's not allowed, and you do it anyway.' I've got no tolerance for it.

The oldest, we're putting more responsibility on her. She's eight, she can understand. I'll whip her, my husband will talk. His belt or mine, might be hers. I used to be better when they were small. I could scream and hoot all day long. Soon as they hear his voice, everybody straightens out. I guess God made it that way, yeah.

The most difficult part of the day? Mmm. After work. Because sometimes I have to rush right to school. When I get home, I have to sit with my feet up and the next thing I'll sleep ten, fifteen minutes, and then I can get up and do something. How do I get to work? Two busses. Half an hour, not that long of a ride. Sometimes he cooks, sometimes I cook, we share that, you know. Food shopping? I do, I do. He does the laundry. We have a washer and dryer.

About grandparenting? I think I'm *more* angry now, I think I'm *more* resentful than I've ever been. Why? Because there are things I want to do. For myself. Yes. And I cannot do it with the grandchildren.

People are so selfish today. When I was a child coming up, everyone helped one another. If you were sick, people from the church would come, clean your house, cook your food, run your errands. They made sure you were taken care of. They don't do that today. They don't. I'm having a problem with the church now, and I don't go as often as I used to. I'd rather preach to homeless people.

What I mean, when it's time to study, I can't because of the kids. I don't know what to do, because when I get home my husband's had them all day and he's tired of it. Right. So if it's a Tuesday or a Thursday, and I get home by five, half an hour I gotta be gone. I haven't had a chance to do homework. [I do it] on the bus. And sometimes I would have the kids with me [in class.]

Where do I get the energy from? I don't know. I have to say the Lord. [With] my husband…[eyes welling up, head bowed, sobbing]. It was a problem, a problem. He was so jealous. God had done so much [for me], people couldn't believe it when they saw me.

I see the failures, the inadequacy, my own shortcomings. I don't see the achievements, no, no, no. I know the Lord has brought me a long way. They used to say I'd be dead in a week, that's how bad I was. So when I look at myself, sometimes I can see the beauty, I can see God. But my husband, he used to hit me. And I fought him back one time. I threw hot water on him.

I think he's proud of me now. I couldn't get along [without him.] No, I don't tell him that, [but] I say, 'Thank you.' I'm afraid to say, 'Oh, honey, you're doing such a wonderful job.' Because my husband, he could be crawling for a week tomorrow. So I'm afraid. You know what I mean? I don't want to let him know I'm so dependent on him, that's it, that's it. Then he'll realize all the power he has, and if he wants to take off on a binge, if he wants to disappear for a week, three weeks, I don't know, I don't know. If I don't do it, where they going to be? Cause there is nobody else.

And you know Sowana just got blessed. She got a scholarship at the Ballet School. She started last week. I was so happy, I was crying. Cause I couldn't afford to do it. You know, [give her] the things I miss in my own life.

What's my strongest support outside of my religion? No one. I don't talk to anybody. No neighbor. No girlfriend. Been through the girlfriend thing. I have been so torn apart, so hurt, so humiliated, so disrespected in the church that it's…oh my God. That's why I don't need no girlfriends.

I talk to my sister sometimes. And I love my pastor. But she's so busy these days. And most people feel if you show any sign of weakness, it's like, *oh, she's cracking up, she's losing it.* So gotta talk to God.

You can't be *any* kind of way, can't say *any* kind of thing, not when you claim the name of Christ. That's why I say, [if] I'm smoking, I can not be preaching. If the Lord said to preach, I would go down to Penn station and preach. I would do it, you know? But I have to get clean.

My daughter's at my house right now. She came yesterday for Thanksgiving. She's in a lesbian relationship, and she knows where I'm at with that. Totally against it. My daughter, she was angry that I left her, that I sent her to live with…. She's not angry now. [But] she's a drug addict. You know the mentality? It's terrible. They're not responsible people. Could care less [about her five kids]. I mean, it's like *thank God I don't have to do it*, that's how she feels. She's incapable. I mean the heart has to really change for that, so I'm waiting for the change.

What do I want to pass on to my grandkids? One: Love God. Two: Love thy neighbor as thyself. Jesus did that. Three: Love your family. What values do I give them? Show patience. Somebody who's made you mad and hurt you, I try, really, really try not to say anything. I start cleaning. I don't curse. I don't want the grandkids to hear, you know what I mean? I don't badmouth in front of the kids. But I'm a little sarcastic sometimes. And I have to catch myself

You got to love through the hurt. That's the greatest thing.

You got to love no matter what. When the person is intolerable, you got to love them. It's the greatest thing that God could love me through the drugs, the prostitution. Oh my God! That's just unbelievable. I was a mess. I was a mess! And God had such pity, such mercy. I picked up diseases, I mean everything, I had everything at the same time. Syphilis and gonorrhea and chlamydia. Oh my God.

When I went to Clinton, Clinton Institute for Women is what it's called, it was terrible. I had eighteen months. In Caldwell, I used to go back and forth for years, ten years. Caldwell Correctional Center. Drugs were available, sure. [But] whenever I went to jail, I just wanted to rest. I didn't want to get high.

How am I going to keep my grandchildren from getting caught in the same way?

I have to pray. What else can you do? Some of the best have gotten caught, snared. That's all you can do is pray. You introduce them to ways and means, you know, a better way.

My oldest granddaughter is not very argumentative, she doesn't like to fight. The next one, she's the fighter, very stubborn. She cheats at games and doesn't keep her room clean. We have two, well actually three bedrooms. To discipline them I call their names to get their attention. One says, 'Yeah, she did it first, she did it first, and that's why I did it.' [Then] I usually take something out of the bible that they know.

[Raising them], I was scared to death. Because I didn't have mothering, I didn't have parenting skills. I didn't have that. I couldn't even remember how to change a diaper. You know what I'm saying? I did not know anything. And I guess the Lord helped me along the way. With their homework, my husband and I, we both help.

For a grandparent in the same situation, I'd say this. Think it through. Because it is a *great* sacrifice of your life. The people you think you can rely on, no more. It's not easy, it's not easy. On a day-to-day basis, I would say the strength comes from God. The energy comes from God. The ability to do comes from God, you know what I mean?

I don't feel like I achieved my own goal that I set. That's college. That's my dream. To go back to classes to get my degree."

According to a full page ad in *The New York Times* by Partnership for a Drug-Free America, "the average age of first-time drug use among teens is thirteen. Some kids start at nine." This ad titled **The Power of a Grandma**, tells grandparents to "use your power as an influence to steer your grandchildren away from drugs."

Keisha is doing that every single day. As a drug free, working woman striving for a college degree, she is showing her grandkids *by example* the value of education, work, and love. That's a lesson the mean streets can't easily drown out. Going from drug addict and prostitute to college student and grandma raising four grandkids is a stunning achievement.

That it is possible is a tribute to a tough lady who looks like Halle Berry and refuses to sing the blues.

Recently, New Jersey has considered the plight of people raising their grandchildren, proposing a $10 million program to give **$250** a month per child to the neediest. This could affect 7400 children. If *unrelated* foster parents raise children, they could qualify for about **$400** a month. Grandparents who need the aid would have to undergo background checks and agree to a new kind of legal guardianship which the state has to create. For grandparents in desperate circumstances, like Keisha, this could mean a brighter future.

Keisha is teetering on the edge. Now that she's drug free, working, and in college, financial assistance could provide the boost she needs to make it all work.

SMART TIPS FROM KEISHA

When life is good and you're finally doing the things you missed, you don't want to take on the job of raising grandchildren.

Think it through. It's a great sacrifice.

But if your child is on drugs, it's your responsibility to step in.

When a grandchild is born addicted, you have to take pity and do your best.

Don't be selfish. Don't say, 'No, I can't take them, I'm working and going to college.'

Pray that God will find some means to help you.

Manage your money by doing much with little. Work to pay off your bills

Find programs that provide childcare benefits and allow you to work.

Check out what the state has to offer grandparents who are raising grandchildren.

Go to school and get certification for a good job with health benefits.

Ask your professor to write a letter for you and apply for financial aid.

Divide household tasks with your husband—cooking, food shopping, laundry.

Enjoy inexpensive activities with your grandkids: television, videos and games.

Accept that sometimes you'll feel angry and resentful, cut off from friends.

Apply for scholarships for your grandchildren.

You've got to love through the hurt. That's the greatest thing.

When you're torn apart and humiliated, talk to someone: your sister or your pastor.

Do homework on the bus, bring the grandkids to class. Show them the value of education.

Teach your grandchildren to love God and love their family.

Don't give up on your dream.

In the next chapter, you'll meet **JUANITA**, a very lucky Hispanic grandmother who adores taking care of her grandchildren. Like Keisha, she works in a department store. But that's where similarities in their backgrounds end.

8

JUANITA

❖

It's Our Tradition

JUANITA, 59, came to the USA in 1956 from a little town in Spain called Orense, near Galicia. She was fifteen. Two years later, at seventeen, she married a boy from Newark, New Jersey. Today, she is the mother of a married daughter, 32, and a married son, 40. She has been a widow for seven years.

Her short, gray hair frames an honest face, clean of makeup. She's wearing blue jeans, a pink velour pullover, and tiny pearl earrings. We sit down to talk at her kitchen table, and her little grandson who is three curls up in her lap. He's blowing bubbles though the straw in his glass of chocolate milk and holding the orange lollypop I've brought him.

This is a three-generation home. Juanita and her husband bought the neat frame house 37 years ago. Now she owns it, and her daughter, son-in-law, and grandson live with her. It's a way of life for this Hispanic family. They *expect* grandparents to be very involved with their grandchildren. "It's our tradition," she says. Juanita's son, a successful attorney in a prestigious law firm, used to spend every weekend at *his* grandparents' house when he was a kid. And now his two children, a seven-year-old boy and a little girl seventeen months, spend two days a week with *their* grandmother.

Juanita has a very busy schedule. She's takes care of all three of her grandchildren and she holds down a full time job. How does she do it?

"To me, it's the normal way of life," she shrugs. "Normal." And her bright smile emphasizes her pleasure. This grandmother has a routine and she follows it.

"My daughter works part-time, four days a week, from 8:30 to 12:30. So I'm responsible for my grandson in the mornings. Plus I take care of my son's two children on Tuesday and Wednesday. And if I'm cooking on Sunday, they'll all come over. Not every Sunday, it gets to be too much. I still have my Mom and Dad, they live nearby. Mom's 82 and Dad's 81, he still drives. And my sister, of course, is always included. And so are my nieces. I used to take care of them when they were little. I called them my Second Generation Kids. It's the Spanish values to feel close to the family. I want them to be there for each other, that's how I feel. My family's pretty close.

I think my husband had the most to do with it. He was the center of everybody. Everybody went to him with a problem. This is hard to say...my father should have been the head of the family, but I think my husband was. And now I think it passed on to me a little. But since my son is getting older, they might go to him. I'm very proud of him. Of both my kids. I sent him to law school and my daughter got a Bachelor in Fine Arts. She works in a print shop.

The Spanish culture is that families just stay together. It was a tradition every Sunday to go to my mother's house. She can't do it any more, so I try to do it maybe once a month. With taking care of the children and working full time, I just can't do it every Sunday.

With my daughter and me [living] in the same house, I assume whatever I do is fine. Well, maybe [I'm] giving too many treats, that seems to be my problem. But my grandson's a good eater. Discipline? Very rarely do we ever give him a little thing in the behind. I was never a spanker, my kids never got spanked. My husband, never, never, never. And they had more respect for him than I can imagine. It could be the love he had for them. There was never a bad voice for the kids. Only once, when my son closed the door and kicked it and my husband said, 'Don't you ever close that door again!' And that was the end of it. They were both obedient children.

I'm working a 38 hour week, full time with benefits. Working ten years. Before that I didn't work. What happened, my husband got sick and he was worried about me. No, not financially. He was in maintenance. He had his own business, he was the owner. He did okay. But he was worried about me emotionally. Psychologically. And he encouraged me to go to work. He hated it! He hated it! He encouraged me, and he hated it. Because he never let me work, it was part of the Spanish culture. He works and I stay home with the kids and take care of the house. Dinner would be on the table at six on the dot. I didn't have to call them.

He was worried about me because I married him at seventeen, and how would I survive? He came to see me once at work and he said, 'I'll never come again.' I work at Customer Service. It bothered him that I was working, that I wasn't home. He said, 'When I come home, I want you to pay attention to me.' He died of cancer a week before our first grandchild was born. I was a young widow, 52.

Working helped. Going to work keeps your mind off of it. And I had a new grandson. I used to get him on the weekends and keep him for a day, and that helped. My daughter wasn't married, it was very hard on her, losing her Dad. We sort of helped each other.

Now I'm a full time working woman and a full time baby sitter. *Two* full time jobs if you add it up. Four mornings a week here. And then my granddaughter, she comes to me Tuesday night and stays here overnight to Wednesday night, another 24 hours. I drive her to my son's house Wednesday, and I wait for my grandson to come home from school, about 3:15. Then I'm there for him.

Where do I get my energy?

I don't know. So far I'm in good health. I can put in full time at work and another 40 hours with the kids. I go to work at one, and I come home ten o'clock. Then eleven or twelve I go to sleep. For fun, I like to shop. I'm in a huge mall, so I find time. If I'm not cooking Sunday, then I'll do some shopping.

Girlfriends? Not really. I have a neighbor, we actually went on a bus trip together. We went to Newport, Rhode Island. It was fun. The family managed without me.

When my husband died, I was financially secure. He took good care of me. I own this house and I own a vacation house, a townhouse down the shore in Cape May. The kids like to go there. And I own a six-family house in Newark, Down Neck. I rent it and get an income. Financially, I'm fine.

I don't know any grandmothers who are angry or resentful [saying] why should I be doing this? I kind of looked forward to being with the kids. I was always a children's lover. I wanted three, they didn't come.

When the two grandkids are both here, I'm trying to keep them from killing each other. She loves him and she follows him around. She wants to play with something and all of a sudden he wants it. When my children leave their kids with me, it's my problem. I do not call them, I do not ask them how to discipline. I take over, and that's that. They respect that, they do not correct me. I wouldn't call them at work unless it was *really* an emergency. Sick or well, it doesn't really matter. A fever of 105? That's high, then I call. I don't take them to the doctor, and I don't go to school. No, these are the parents' responsibilities. I'm doing this because I want to, that's it. Just for the love of the grandchildren. And to help my kids, I think.

Everybody works. Husbands, wives. My son would survive fine, my daughter-in-law doesn't have to work. She *likes* to work, to have her own money, for her own independence. My husband would have been offended, yes, he would have. It was part of the culture that the wife doesn't work. With my daughter, she *needs* to work. They would have to hire a baby sitter. Or she would have to cut back quite a bit, a financial drain. So I'm providing that kind of care. It gives me pleasure to know that.

Sometimes I get tired. And I figure, well, I can rest on the weekend. My grandson is here, he's an easy child. But he's a child. He runs up, he runs down, he's all over the place. But he's not hard to take care of.

At work, I'm on my feet from one until we close at 9:30. It's hard dealing with people sometimes. But it's not physically hard. You get used to it. My job, it's pleasant most of the time. Sometimes it's stressful, [but] it's not too bad. I like my job. It's a twenty minute drive home, that's all it is. I was never afraid to drive home at night.

I feel my children are depending on me, that's the way I look at it. And I like that feeling.

I don't go to church. No, I'm not a churchgoer. I'm not a practicing Catholic. I used to be, not anymore. I believe in God, I just don't believe that much in the church anymore. I was never that big of a religious person. I don't believe Jesus is going to save me. No, no, it's not a religious obligation to mind my grandchildren.

Basically, the family is it! Outside of the family circle, there's acquaintances. But they're not people I'd go to, not in an emergency. The family is it. And I don't feel I'm taken advantage of, no. I'm doing it because I want to. They would love me even if I couldn't take care of their kids.

Sometimes I give them a little grandmotherly advice. Yes, I have, I have. A little bit, not too much. Because, it's their children, they should raise them. But I have said, 'Well, maybe you should do this or that.' Whether they follow it or not, most of the time they don't. I don't feel insulted, no. It's up to them. They would not be disrespectful.

I can tell my daughter, 'You should do this, you shouldn't do that.' But it's no big deal. She wouldn't say, 'Stay out of it, it's none of your business.' I try to be respectful of their privacy. Yes. Because they are a family, a husband and wife. Also, most of the time when they're here, I'm not, because I'm working. So that works out. I leave a quarter-to-one and I don't come home until after ten. So like they have the house.

And in the morning there's nobody here but my grandson and me. Not too many opportunities to clash.

My coping skills? I don't know. I think you just show a lot of love, that's what it is. **Show that the grandchildren are your first priority**. And the children feel that, yeah. Between a daughter and a mother there have to be tangles—oh, definitely. How do we settle? We just ignore it. Not a problem because we have the same values about the house and we try to be forgiving. I try to be easygoing, tolerant. People irritate each other, oh yes. My daughter irritates me lots of times. I let it blow over and forget about it. When it's over, it's over, and that's the end of it. I don't hold grudges. It's over, forget it, let go of it.

I work three evenings, so if my daughter needs to go to work or she has plans, I can switch. That's not a problem, I have flexibility. We accommodate to each other, yes, we do. And my manager likes me, so I can switch with other people.

When I went away with my neighbor, my daughter was happy for me to go. We take vacations together down to Cape May. Usually a week or two. They don't go away without the child, they take him, and he's got Grandma. How do you develop this kind of closeness? I don't know. It just happens.

Now my daughter is moving out of this house. I never really asked them to move. As far as I was concerned, they were here to stay. Her husband wants his own home, which is understandable. When you get married you need your own home, so I don't see anything wrong with that. I didn't say anything one way or another [when] they bought a house. It's only fair they have their own house. No matter what, this is still the mother-in-law's house. My son-in-law said they were going shopping and they looked about two years. They bought the house a year ago and they're fixing it up.

It's close. Two minutes. You could walk in nice weather, yeah. It will change the pattern. It will be harder for her, it won't make a difference to me. She has to get him dressed and bring him here. But I don't think it will be a strain. My daughter never had an outside person, no never. She would never ask an outsider to take care of her son. We stick to the family. It's a little sad they're moving, but they have to. It's only fair. It will be better for them."

When Juanita's daughter steps into the kitchen, I ask her how she'd rate her mother *as a grandparent*.

"You mean on a scale of one to ten?" she asks, grinning. "Ten!" she explodes. Then she turns to her mother, clearly teasing her. "As a mother? Maybe a one." And they giggle together like two girlfriends.

SMART TIPS FROM JUANITA

It's the Spanish tradition to be involved with your grandchildren, so you look forward to doing the job.

Taking care of your grandchildren is a *normal* way of life.

To be a close family and to be there for each other are values we pass on.

Do not spank your grandchildren. Show them the love you have for them.

A full time job helps emotionally to get through the pain of becoming a widow.

Taking care of your grandchildren takes your mind off your grief.

If your husband provided for your financial security, this reduces the stress.

Be flexible and try to accommodate your work schedule so you can help with the grandchildren.

Take full responsibility for your grandchildren when you mind them. Don't call the parents at work except in an emergency.

Don't take over your children's parental responsibilities.

Mind your grandchildren because you *love* them, not out of religious obligation or duty.

When you take care of grandchildren, you are also helping your child financially because they don't have to pay babysitters.

The family is it! You go to them, not outsiders, for emotional support.

Your grandchildren are your first priority.

Be respectful of your children's privacy when you live together. Remember they are a family.

When you live in the same house, reduce opportunities for clashes.

Ignore tangles. Be easygoing and tolerant.

Try to forgive. Let arguments blow over and forget it. Don't hold grudges.

Limit your grandmotherly advice because it's their children and they should raise them.

Don't feel insulted if your child decides to move out.

Understand their desire to have their own home.

JUANITA, healthy and energetic, is one of millions of working grandparents. Many are helping to raise their grandchildren while holding down part-time or full-time jobs. A front page article in *The New York Times* (November 26, 2003) reports that William D. Novelli, the chief executive of AARP, with 35 million members, says, "a majority of AARP members still work."

In the next chapter, you will hear from another grandfather. Unlike **LIN** in Chapter 5, this grandfather did not leave his homeland to become a nanny, and he didn't move into his child's home. **DAVID** and his wife live in their own home only a few miles from their grand-children's home. **DAVID** is retired, so he has plenty of time on his hands. Here's what he decided to do about that.

9

DAVID

✦

I'm Retired and Available

He is a tall, robust man over six feet, with a full head of thick gray hair and mischievous blue eyes. A solid figure wearing a slate blue sweater, he fills the room with his energy. He's a man who can joke and laugh at himself, likable and upbeat.

DAVID, 76, is married 51 years. His son, 46, is a busy pediatrician, and his daughter, 37, is married to a geriatric psychiatrist. He earned a degree as an accountant, but he never practiced because his father needed help in his struggling firm assembling lighting fixtures.

"We made a living," he says. "But in 1995, I wasn't paid by my customers, and I couldn't pay my suppliers. So I filed [for] bankruptcy." His wife worked as an IBM operator until they had children. "Two wonderful kids."

What David regrets is that *his* children never had grandparents to go to. His voice turns plaintive and a sadness creeps in. "They were old and sick, they couldn't play with them or give them much attention."

And that's why he feels so motivated to be a wonderful, close grandfather. To make up for his children's loss. Here's how he explains it.

"In the light of what they missed, it was incumbent upon me to try to offer some type of closeness, the feeling that my children never had. Put it this way: I wanted to do it. Nothing like *my* childhood. I had a very ill grandmother in Brooklyn and I lived in the Bronx. I took the train by myself, I was seven or eight, to spend the weekend. And I enjoyed it. I have fond memories.

My retirement didn't mark the beginning of taking over as a grandparent, no. Even before that, I started taking afternoons off and coming home early. When my daughter-in-law said, 'Can you pick Bobby up after school?' I said, 'Of course.' And I tried to be available for him at that time. I was slowing down, and I made it a point that if I promised him I'd be there at a certain time, I'd be there. I kind of eased into it a little bit at a time.

And I want to say something else. *My own children, I didn't see them grow up because of my working hours.* I worked 4:30 in the morning to 8:00 at night. In your own business, you don't count the hours. I was remiss. My wife raised my kids. Here's a funny story we used to laugh about. When I walked home [early] one afternoon, my daughter was home and she looked at my wife and said, "Who's he?"

Well things were different then, you worked very long hours. **I didn't have much time with my kids. And now I want to get another shot at it.** That's right. And it helps me keep out of trouble. I won't stay home and fight with my wife.

For one thing, we had Bobby a lot of the time. And then gradually I worked in that I'm not only available for him, but also if his brother needs help in getting some place, I can do that too. Now I'm waiting for my granddaughter to grow up to offer my services. My son has these three, two boys and a girl.

Bobby is the oldest and he's into hockey. I know that my son is working and my daughter-in-law is also working. She's an ophthalmologist. They are two hard working doctors, very committed parents, and very committed to their professions. So if I can ease it for them, I'm available. I do it, no questions asked.

As a matter of fact, the second boy is into soccer, so I take him where he has to be. And Bobby goes to hockey practice twice a week. He goes to the sports arena at Montclair State. So I drive him. I wait for the practice to be over, and I bring him home. The practice is two hours. Then there are games on the weekend, there are travel games. We went to Connecticut overnight. We went to Chimney Rock Ice Skating Arena off Route 22. Various locations. We went down to Bridgewater last Sunday.

He has to travel, and my son is working or he's tired. And look, I'm available and I don't mind, and he's a wonderful boy. He's fourteen and the younger boy is ten and the little girl, she'll be six. Mostly I'm involved with the two boys. Maybe she's more preferential to the female, she's close to my wife.

A funny story. About a month ago, Bobby had to be in Connecticut, a weekend session, Saturday and Sunday. If they won the Sunday morning game, they'd have a play-off game Sunday night. I picked him up and we went to Connecticut for the Saturday night game. He played his game and we came back that night to the hotel. And I told him, 'Listen, Bobby, I got to leave early in the morning for a 50th anniversary party in Philadelphia.' My son would drive up.

I drove back to New Jersey at five a.m. to pick up my wife. And it was a glaze of ice on the road, and I was going twenty miles an hour till I hit Danbury. Then it turned to rain and I got home nine in the morning, and we made it to Philly. Thank God it all worked out. My son got up there in time. They won the first game Sunday and they had the playoff. I have great pride in this grandson, I certainly do.

I always taught him one thing. I said, 'Bobby, when you shake hands with a person, mean it. Be firm. Don't break his hand, but be firm.' And he breaks my hand now! He remembers that. Not only that, I told him, 'Smile. People like to see a smiling face.' I said, 'Don't be miserable, life is worth living, whatever will be, will be. But smile!'

I've been telling him jokes. He has a good sense of humor, yes, he does. I'd set him up on the old family routine. 'Bobby, did you take a bath last night?' And he's say, 'Why?' And I'd say, 'Because we're missing the bathtub.' Or, 'Do you know Lincoln's Gettysburg Address?' And he's say, 'I didn't even know he moved.'

When we go out, do I pay or do [my children] pay? Oh, no, no, no, they have very weak arms, they start to tremble and put their hands in their pockets. I pay the bills. If we go out to eat locally, I usually pay.

Vacations? I will say this. We go to Florida sometimes. We rent a suite where *both* families would come, my daughter too, of course. And the kids love each other. I think it's wonderful they want to be with their parents and grandparents. It's a big clannish family, all the cousins. My daughter has three boys. Triplets.

And my wife will send Meals-On-Wheels to my daughter-in law because she doesn't have time to prepare. My wife has the time and the ability and the strength, so she cooks and I bring it over the same night. I drop it off. They call me Pop. I deliver it and I never get a tip.

Do I discipline them? No, it's up to the parents to discipline. In my presence they act the way I want them to act. Out of fear, or with respect, I don't know. I will say, 'Don't do this, you're going to hurt yourself.' But I don't discipline. I try to keep them in line. I have no problems with these kids, they're good kids. I get the welcome and they're affectionate, yeah. There would have to be a great infraction, but I've never been confronted with it.

I've always maintained…I've always tried to have a sense of humor and break up the tension. When people are having a serious conversation on religion or politics, I'll interject a joke, that's my contribution. My contention is I'd rather have a thousand friends than one enemy. And I try to say hello to strangers all over the place. Bobby looks at me and he says, 'You know him, Pop?' And I say, 'No. What's wrong with saying *Hi* to a person you don't know?' I think it's a model for him. I say to him, 'That's the way I am.' He's an outgoing kid.

As a matter of fact, I even pick him up at school. Instead of riding the bus and wasting an hour before he gets home, I pick him up and he's home in ten minutes. So he has extra time to relax or do homework. I tell him the night before if I'll be there. He knows where the car is and I'll park the car at the appointed place and walk over to the front door to greet him as he comes out. With the younger boy, I have nothing to do with picking up. No. So far it's Bobby.

Jealousy? The younger one, he's made some comments about coming to [his] sports events. So I've been trying to take him to basketball practice at night at Seton Hall. I try to do it. How much can you do? My daughter says, 'The kids are playing soccer this Sunday. You want to come down to see them?' A two hour trip. You do these things.

Several weeks ago, the younger boy made a comment. He said, 'I hope I become a grandparent the way my grandparents are.' And that was an overwhelming statement for a kid that age. I think it's great. I'm a very wealthy man when it comes to family, the love and affection.

A crisis? Yes. There were illnesses in the family where we all rallied around. We were available to them, they needed us. My son had an illness that was very drastic, and we all pitched in. It was a family affair, [we are] family oriented. A person needs help, you're there. Thank God I have good health. I have a certain amount of financial security.

Help them with homework? Not really. Because they know so much more than I do. This week I was waiting for Bobby to get ready for practice and the younger boy was doing vocabulary on a multiple choice basis, so we did it together. But he knew the answers, I wasn't much help. On a weekly basis, how much time do I put in? Driving to the games and other things? I can't pinpoint the hours. Three hours round trip for a game, two hours to school. I get there early, I don't like to rush.

My wife takes them shopping. Banana Republic and Bloomingdale's. But heck, that's part of it. You see them enjoy it. I buy them video games at Toys-R-Us, hi tech games and Barbie dolls. Am I spoiling them? My son says I do. I was never spoiled, and it's just too bad my children were never spoiled by their grandparents, they didn't have that opportunity. So I'll spoil them! If they want something and I have the means, I'm going to give it. I want to see that smile on their face.

You know, people leave wills. I want to *see* them appreciate things. Sometimes you revolt when you see the prices, how hard it was for you to save a buck, so you resent the fact. But overall, I'd say I like to see them have it. I close my eyes if they really want it. But I tell them, 'Listen, that's too expensive.' And with the triplets, you gotta buy three! And they have so much, it's ridiculous. But they're enjoying it and they look forward to going to Toys-R-Us.

I don't bathe the kids or put them to bed. I do the things that generate a lot of fun and appreciation. I'm mostly the chauffeur, the driver, I see they make their appointments. I'm at the school, at their sports events.

Do I give my children advice? I've expressed my thoughts sometimes. Nothing to embarrass them, but I'll give them some advice, take it or leave it. Sometimes they see the light, and sometimes they say, 'Hey, it's my kid, I'll raise them the way I want.' I accept that absolutely.

Emotionally, I've got my two feet on the ground. And I've got health and money. There are families today where the mother and father work and the kids are on their own most of the time. I've been fortunate all around. I wake up in the morning, I say, 'God, I'm up! I got another day! I'm alive!'

My main fault is I do not do housework and most of my fights with my wife are about housework. I was lucky working 4:30 to eight at night. Now I can sleep when I want to, [but] I'm up at 5:30. I'll do shopping, food shopping, but no cooking. I don't cook, and I don't do floors and windows. A bone of contention. I avoid arguments by running out of the house. 'I got Bobby to take care of.' A little respite. My wife doesn't drive, so I do the driving. If she has to go to Bloomingdale's, I sit in the car for an hour. I'm a great sitter. I have patience. I listen to the radio.

My wife and me, we go away on vacation. We went on a cruise to Alaska, it was great. We go to Atlantic City, we sleep overnight, it's a break in the routine. I like television, I record almost every show, every movie. I have a collection of videos, three, four thousand, maybe more.

My grandchildren go to private school. Me? We lived in an inner city where all our friends were within a radius of three, four blocks, and we'd get together on street corners and joke and talk, a convivial atmosphere. I'm still friends with people from the Bronx for sixty years. I don't know if you have that today. I drive them everywhere. And if I got an appointment, something I have to do, I say, 'I'm not available.' I've done that, certainly. If there's a time we want for ourselves.

Coping skills? Maybe it was in my background from when I was a kid. I went to my grandparents as often as I could, and maybe it rubbed off on me. There was that warmth. My grandmother was very old with asthma, and she had attacks. I choke up when I think about it. Yeah, I saw by example certain moral values, absolutely. The fact that family comes first. My father, my uncles, they did everything they possibly could.

If my grandkids could pick that up, I'd be grateful. If they could just know that life is a battle, but come up smiling. Be friendly, it's easy, very easy, people want to be friendly with you. What's important? The ten commandments, basically, and what they learn in school.

I have mixed emotions that they go to a religious school. Of course, they're missing a lot of down-to-earth, practical stuff like on-the-streets type of life. They're being protected. To me, a parochial school, you're being protected and when they get out, maybe they'll get hurt by facing life. I don't know.

Unfortunately, my wife and I are not religious. We don't practice. But we are for Israel, for the Jewish people. But organized religion? No. If atheism had holidays, we'd be atheists.

It doesn't disturb us that our grandkids are being raised in a religious atmosphere. No, no, not at all. Somebody has to carry on the traditions of Judaism. But we ourselves? No. I'll go to services. I've forgotten how to read Hebrew I'm embarrassed to say, but I go and I feel a certain warmth with the music and the intonations of the prayers. Touching my roots. But I don't participate in organized religion. Whatever I feel, I carry in my heart.

You know the story about the author who wrote a book on atheism? And then he prayed to God he sells it!

Bobby is the only one I have a relationship with because of his age. But I try to joke and tell him practical things, the reality of things. I mean sometimes he doesn't even talk to me in the car. He's tired and I don't want to butt into his dreams. But on an overall basis, we talk all the time. I'll interject a certain remark that I think he should listen to. Whether he follows it or not, it's up to him. He's mentioned [personal] things to me, and I've said, 'Listen, that's up to your parents.' He's got to obey them. They're the parents. I make that very clear.

And he's very close to my daughter, he loves his aunt. I hear he had a conversation with her and he said, 'You know I don't know what I'm going to do if anything happens to Gogi and Pop.' I wouldn't want him to feel that attached. God forbid, something does happen, he'll lose himself. But I think that's a helluva expression.

I've been grandparenting over fifteen years, so I have some tips. Don't butt in. But be available to them. You can guide them to a certain point, but leave most of it to the parents. Be available if they need help. Simple as that.

Do I worry about drugs and violence, the sex on television? I'm dead set against the horror shows and the violence and the exposure of sex. I'll tell you a story.

A very embarrassing moment happened on the trip to Connecticut. We went back to the hotel and I'm playing with the TV and there's an X-rated movie. And Bobby said, 'Wowee!' And I shut it off immediately. I said, 'Let's go down and eat.' And while we were eating, he said, 'I'm full. I'm going up to the room.' He came back five minutes later. *They blocked the channel.* At fourteen, a normal reaction. I was embarrassed.

I give him movies, some of the old movies I've collected, what I thought was terrific. Appropriate for him like *Stalag 17* with William Holden. And he loves it. 'You got any more like that?' And I've taken them to the movies when they had a day off from school. Bobby's seen a lot of my Hitchcock movies: *Rear Window* and *The Birds*.

Good times. Good memories."

SMART TIPS FROM DAVID

If you have fond memories of being with your own grandparents, you'll want to give your grandchildren that experience.

If you didn't spend much time with your own children, grandparenting gives you another shot at it.

Being the driver and taking your grandchildren to sporting events and appointments eases the strain on their hardworking parents.

Teach your grandchildren how to shake hands, how to smile, and that life is worth living.

Tell them jokes. Encourage them to have a sense of humor.

Take family vacations together. The grandchildren will enjoy being with their cousins.

Send home-made-meals to their house if the parents are too busy to cook.

Do not discipline your grandchildren. This is up to their parents.

If you can pick up a grandchild at school and save an hour ride on the school bus, do it.

In the car, you have an opportunity to enjoy conversations and warm exchanges.

When you spend more time with one grandchild than another, be sensitive to jealousy.

If your grandchildren appreciate what you do, they will want to be loving grandparents.

Be family oriented. If anyone needs help or a crisis occurs, rally round them.

Take the family out to enjoy a meal together, and pick up the bill.

Spoil your grandkids. Toys and video games will put a smile on their face.

You can give advice about parenting, but accept absolutely that your children will raise their kids the way they want.

Be grateful for every day you have health and money.

Take time out for yourself for vacations with your spouse.

Enjoy a hobby, like collecting old movies. Share them with your grandchildren.

Pass on the moral values you experienced as a child.

Accept that your grandchildren attend religious school, even if you are not religious.

Teach your grandchildren practical things so they avoid getting hurt.

Don't butt into your grandchildren's dreams.

Guide them, but leave the parenting to the parents.

It is interesting that both grandfathers, **LIN** and **DAVID,** do not share their grandchildren's religious beliefs. Yet each one shows respect and tolerance and neither grandfather interferes. Another attitude they agree on is that family comes first. However, on other issues, spending money and spoiling their grandkids, they are worlds apart.

In the next chapter, you will meet **MARILYN.** Almost a decade ago, her daughter was divorced and had two small children to raise. That's when Marilyn stepped in, juggling grandparenting with her full time job as a school teacher.

10

MARILYN

❋

She was a Divorced, Single Mom

She speaks deliberately, like a school teacher. It was her profession for thirty years. She tells me she retired only three weeks ago. She has just come from the beauty salon on this rainy Friday morning as we sit down to talk.

MARILYN, 67, is a small, sweet faced woman, wearing a navy blue sweatsuit. She has two children. "My son lives in San Diego, California. He's married fifteen years, but no kids. My daughter lives close by. She's 45 and her two kids are now teenagers."

"Wait," she says. "Before we begin the interview, I have a *personal story* of my own to tell." Her story is poignant and goes back to when her husband, a CPA, was making $32.50 a week. "My mother died when my kids were four and three, so they never really knew their grandmother. And my father, I seldom saw him after she died. So my kids were deprived."

At that time, Marilyn made a decision. She would do everything she could to see that *her grandchildren* would have a close relationship to her. She would be the grandmother her kids never had.

"I think it's so important. It's essential to good health. I wouldn't let my grandchildren be deprived of that. They live about a twenty minute ride away and I see them frequently. I took on the job even *before* my daughter's divorce.

I'd come home from work three, three-thirty and go over to their house to see what they needed and to help with the baby. I was teaching full time. I taught a multitude of grades and I did Title I, that's remediation.

My daughter worked the very morning of the day the baby was born and she went back to work immediately. She had a full time housekeeper, but I felt I wanted to be very close to them. So I'd go over almost every day after school. Her husband was in his own business, they did carpet cleaning.

My granddaughter is almost seventeen now and my grandson is almost fifteen. But at the time of the divorce, the children were six and eight. I'd go there to help, and I'd say, 'Take some time, meet a friend for lunch. Go and let me spend time with the children.' She seldom took time off, she was a determined professional, a CPA. She had many housekeepers over the years, but they came and went.

It was tough on them. And well, we've helped over the years financially. Her ex-husband contributes very little. He's required by law to give a certain amount each month which he does, and he takes them out to dinner and buys them clothes. He's a phenomenal golfer, so if they want golf or tennis lessons he's willing. He hasn't remarried.

With her divorce, I focused more carefully on my grandchildren. If they needed something in the market, or getting the kids back and forth to where they had to go, dancing lessons, tennis, I did it. How did I pack it all in? I picked up some prepared food and brought it to their house. Or I'd say, 'Come over, I'll make dinner, eat here.'

During their school vacations, we tried to take them to different places. We still do that. February we'd take them skiing. I'd sit in the lodge and they'd ski up in the Catskills in New York. Last April, the whole family went to Disney World. And we went to California. We tried to expose them to different places. We'd take them to museums and planetariums. We even had them to the opera, *La Boheme* at the Met, then dinner at Tavern on the Green. A lot of good experiences introducing them to cultural values. They both love today's modern music, but they [should know] there are other music decisions available and wonderful museums. Appreciation makes you happier in the long run.

Even when they were [little], there was the Newark Museum and Morris County Museum and Liberty Science Center. We took them to *Fiddler on the Roof* and other cultural experiences, things that were part of the background of their ancestors.

The divorce was not amicable. Both parents were very bitter, lots of reasons. It's hard to say how it affected the children. It's *got* to affect the kids some way or another. After all, they were close to him.

Now the parents say they didn't work hard enough on the marriage. It's true, yes. But I have to butt out. [That generation was] easy in, easy out. Quick to divorce. There were many problems, but I think possibly they could have worked it out with a little more effort. My task then, when they were six and eight, was just to see they had what they needed. And to [get them] where they needed to be. At a doctor's appointment, I'd do most of the waiting, the preliminary waiting, and my daughter would [arrive] in time to go in with the children. I'd pick them up at school and get them there. I'd pick up my grandson at school and take him for a haircut or to his friend's house.

There was anxiety about how the kids would be affected by the divorce. Their father wasn't around a great deal of the time. Now the parents are easier, and it's a lot better. They call each other, they're friendly, they help out when one needs a particular favor. It's a lot better in the last few years and they're polite, even though they are not together.

The toughest part was some of the emotional problems that came up, things that bothered the children. They'd have a fight with a friend. [My granddaughter would] come home and say, 'So-and-so has a boyfriend and I liked him.' My grandson has a lot harder time telling me if something's bothering him. My granddaughter, she's open, she'll confide, she trusts me. And she's pretty good with her mother, they do a lot together, shopping, the beauty parlor, girl things.

I think my grandson is close to his mother, but in some way he's fighting for independence. I try not to push him. I say, 'Is there anything I can do for you?' If he says, 'You can pick me up at so-and-so's house,' that's how I get to know his friends.

I was never in a position where I had to defend their father or discuss the divorce. Yes, we've discussed problems over the years. My daughter and I are close. But I never got in the middle. I tried to keep quiet. It's interesting. When my granddaughter was bat mitzvahed, after they had been divorced, they wouldn't even take any pictures together. But two years later, at my grandson's bar mitzvah, they were a lot more relaxed, talking about the kids and so on. It made it a lot easier for the kids. And for me.

Right now my daughter's working very long hours and going to Brooklyn three days a week. There's no limit to her hours, twelve to fourteen hours a day, it's just incredible. She's out of the house early in the morning, and she could come home like eight or nine at night or even later.

My granddaughter calls me in the morning before she goes to school. I pick up certain things for her, I'm in the market almost every day. She'll say, 'Grandma, can you pick up this or that?' The housekeeper makes dinner, and the kids are pretty close to her. But she doesn't drive. She comes in from Brooklyn on Monday evening and goes home Saturday around noon. She does the cooking, the laundry, the cleaning. But I do the shopping. My daughter is a terrific young woman. She calls from the car on the way home from work.

My daughter is seeing someone new. It's more a casual friendship than a serious relationship. That's my feeling anyway. My granddaughter says she could do without him. But my grandson, they'll play ping pong. And [sometimes] he comes with his son, [who is] my granddaughter's age, and they go to Seton Hall basketball games.

Even before the divorce, when her husband was not doing well, we paid for private school and summer camp. Vacations in Florida, we'd pick up the tab completely.

My daughter does very well. [But] it's a large house, and she bought it from her ex-husband. It's difficult to pay the bills: the electric, heating, phone, and utilities. So whatever money she makes, it's an enormous amount to lay out. And we wanted to see that their lives were not disrupted, that they had good things like Tavern on the Green. I felt it was our obligation to contribute financially.

Unfortunately, I've been ill the last couple of years. Which is why I wear this bracelet. I'm sporting two artificial heart valves. Mitral valve and aortic valve, two valve replacements. I sure don't want to lay in bed, that's certain. Last year, I was out of work three months. I must take coumadin which is a very strong drug, I have no choice. I take a lot of medication, that's the reason for this bracelet. My daughter is concerned. She works out at five a.m. and she's very active and, hopefully, healthy.

I think we're good friends. I think she has grown to be probably my closest friend. She doesn't have to tell me her secrets. She knows I'm there whenever she needs me, and as long as I'm physically able to do it, I will. I know I can count on her. And my husband, he backs me up.

I think we have an extended family that's very special. Even if the parents are not together, my grandchildren have two loving parents. They love them and care about them, and I feel we are very fortunate. We have a special relationship with our grandchildren that lots of people don't have. Something in life that you miss if you haven't had that.

The three generation family, I [saw] a lot of it teaching, a great deal, oh yes. Many of the children I worked with [had] single moms. I worked with basic skills children, which means they didn't pass the achievement test. Many in broken homes, drugs, a couple of mothers in jail. Some kids were living with relatives that didn't want them. There were language problems. It was a struggle [to read] English and pass the test. Some were being raised by grandparents, absolutely. Maybe 35% had grandmothers and grandparents in their lives who were looking after them.

There were many single moms who had to work and they were fortunate if they had [a grandparent] to look after their kids. I know grandparents who used to come all the time. The kid got sick [at school], who would come and pick him up? The grandparent. Take him home and give him a little tender loving care. I saw a lot of grandparents being surrogate parents. Yes, absolutely.

There were times my daughter asked me to do something and I really couldn't, and she was upset with me. But I stood my ground. And then she called and apologized, she was sorry. No, I don't feel resentment. I feel blessed that I had the opportunity to know my grandkids. I'm sorry my son and his wife have not had children. I feel lucky that I can be involved, it keeps me young.

With discipline, I back off. I try not to ever go back on what my daughter says. She has the final say, I will never get involved. I will never say in front of the children, 'I don't know why your mother did that,' or 'Why don't you let her go?' I never correct her. I will not belittle what she says. [If they're] being punished and can't go out, I'm not going to let them. I will not interfere. Absolutely not. I carry out what has to be done and I see them almost every day.

If I want to go away for two weeks, a vacation, I say, 'Look, we're going away, you'll have to do without us.' I don't think you should lay guilt on yourself. That's probably the most wasted emotion, guilt. Do what you can. Support your kids in every way possible. And if you can't, just accept it and don't feel guilty. Do not live with guilt.

Sometimes my husband has said that I'm doing too much, that I should give them room to grow. And he may be right. I don't give them enough space sometimes to let them grow away from me. For example, my granddaughter is working on a special science project and she'd manage to get a late bus, [but] I don't give her a chance. Maybe I'm robbing them of their independence and their ability to solve a problem [because] I jump in too fast. With a child who has a single mom, you tend to be a little bit overprotective. I know how busy my daughter is, especially when tax season comes. Nothing is too hard, no day is too long, that's her work ethic.

Now that I'm retired, I'll try to fight for my *own* independence. There are some things I want to do. I want to get involved with New Jersey Performing Arts Center in Newark. I'd like to do some work there once a week, whatever they need me for. I'm joining an investment club of friends. I'd like to spend more time with my sister who's suffering from Alzheimer's.

At holiday time, I feel gypped because my mother wasn't around for my kids. [But] I hope to live a long and healthy life. I want to see my grandchildren grow. It's brought me more pleasure than anything. No matter what life has in store for them, they had a relationship that was very special. It's been a wonderful experience."

Marilyn probably does a lot more than most grandmothers her age. Despite health problems and two heart valve replacements, she is providing something very special to her grandchildren and to her divorced daughter.

With about half of American marriages ending in divorce, the number of single moms has exploded. In many cases, as she observed from her experience as a teacher of thirty years, grandparents, especially grandmothers, take over as best they can.

A *New York Times* article (November 30, 2003) states that, "…about 300,000 children [are] living in grandparent-headed households in New York State, according to the 2000 census. Nationally, that figure is 4.5 million, a 30 percent increase from 1990 to 2000." Many grandparents raising grandchildren are living in poverty and wrestling with problems more critical than the divorce of their child: drugs, mental illness, jail, and violence.

Unlike these grandparent-headed households, Marilyn has the energy, money, and desire to help her daughter and grandchildren. She is a woman who considers herself blessed to be close to them.

SMART TIPS FROM MARILYN

In a bitter divorce, be aware that your grandchildren will be affected.

Focus carefully on your grandchildren, see that their lives are not disrupted.

Never get in the middle. Don't defend one parent or discuss the divorce.

If a single mom is working long hours, help your grandkids get what they need.

Take them to a doctor's appointment, a haircut, a friend's house.

Accept that anxiety and emotional problems will arise.

On your grandchildren's school vacations, take them someplace special.

Introduce them to museums, planetariums, and cultural events.

Do the shopping. Bring prepared food to their house or invite them to dinner.

It's a grandparent's responsibility to contribute financially.

If you can afford it, pay for private schools, summer camp, and vacations.

Even if you have medical problems, be helpful as long as you are physically able.

Don't expect your daughter to tell you her secrets.

When the parents are divorced, having an extended family becomes very special.

If both divorced parents are loving to their children, you are fortunate.

Don't feel resentment when your divorced daughter is upset with you.

Feel blessed you have the opportunity to know your grandchildren.

Raising grandchildren keeps you young.

Never go back on what the parent says. Never correct or belittle the parent.

The most wasted emotion is guilt. Do as much as feels comfortable.

Give your grandchildren room to grow. Don't step in too quickly and rob them of their ability to solve problems.

Take time out to the things you want to do with your spouse.

Grandparenting can bring extraordinary pleasure.

MARILYN brings you the perspective of a well-educated, professional woman with financial security. Of course, not all grandmothers are in such a secure position when their grandchildren are caught in the crossfire of a bitter divorce.

Perhaps you won't agree with everything she says. You may think that her closeness to her grandkids springs more from *her* needs than from theirs. Maybe you would do things differently.

Finally, we come to the last story. In the next chapter, **CHRISTINE,** a long distance grandmother, is struggling to maintain a relationship with her two grandchildren who live thousands of miles away in Singapore and speak Mandarin, the language of their Asian mother. These are difficulties many grandparents are facing today as interracial and intercultural marriages bring new challenges, and long distances separate grandparents from their grandkids.

11

CHRISTINE

✦

Grandkids in Singapore

Her three story brick colonial house is set back from the street about 200 feet. Driving onto the white pebbled circular driveway, you get a view of a four acre estate of majestic old trees and huge rhododendron.

CHRISTINE, 67, is every bit the lady of the house, warm and welcoming. She has a tea service set out for us on a lovely tray with white linen napkins and china cups and saucers. She pours tea from a flowered china kettle, and offers sliced apples, nuts and cookies.

She wears a long navy skirt, a white shirt buttoned to her throat, plus a handsome embroidered ski sweater. A pretty woman, with flawless pale skin, sky blue eyes, and mascaraed lashes, her blonde hair is swept up into a fashionable French knot.

It's March and her garden is still asleep, but you can see sharp outlines of the sculptured flower beds. "Gardening? Me? Oh no," she shakes her head. "I don't do the gardening."

We talk in a cozy glass alcove off an elegant paneled den. Our swivel chairs face each other, with our knees almost touching. She pauses to give thoughtful answers, determined to be precise. She is a visual artist, one of her projects is painting decorative screens.

She has three children, two are married. Her daughter lives around the corner and has three children, ages twelve, nine, and six, so she sees them often. Her son lives in Singapore with his Asian wife and two children. With her son's children, it's quite different. She is a long-distance grandmother. She explains the sharp contrast to her relationships with the other grandchildren.

"I speak to my daughter regularly or leave a message. And my granddaughter calls me a great deal and comes over. The youngest, the six-year-old, she comes to see me. She calls me Nana. They're very busy with school, busy with homework, and that's the worst time to visit, because my daughter's trying to monitor the homework situation. And she's very busy herself, so we'll go out for lunch when the kids are in school and we can talk one-on-one. She's doesn't work outside the home, but she's on the Boards of many things including a bank, and very busy with her responsibilities.

With these grandchildren [living] close by, we do a lot of things together: shopping, movies, TV. And we have a place in Vermont and they've always come there since they were born. A wonderful rendez-vous for [our] family. Something we hold dear. When they're in Vermont [and we] see them having a good time, just popping over to our cabin next door, that's the most fun. They come for a week, here and there, scattered over the summer. But that's changing because the kids are going to camp. I see them less as they get bigger.

It's wonderful to know we are neighbors. When they're not there, when they're away skiing, I don't like it. The oldest is into La Crosse, that's his big deal. They go to Peck, a private school in Morristown. And they take piano lessons. Our chief form of getting together is holidays and sometimes a sports event. I just see them very casually. But for certain things, well…I've gone over every Friday afternoon to take care of one of the children because the others had company. I like to talk to them, I guess that's what I enjoy most. And I hate it when they're fighting.

When they come to visit me, they come the back way, through the fence. My husband made a gate for them. They share the use of our pool. It's a close mother-daughter relationship, but we're not in each other's hair. And I'm very careful, very conscious of that. Being a grandparent to these children is pure joy. But sometimes you're better off if you don't know something. It's a burden sometimes.

Yes, my daughter confides in me and she would feel comfortable talking about a problem. We talk frequently, I think we are good friends, I think we're very close. We don't chat every day, but we have good talks. And that's a great joy to me. I'll drop the little one off and stay for a cup of tea. [But if] we're having dinner together, the four of us, we make a date a month in advance. I think her husband likes me quite a lot, which is nice. I like him too.

My son lives in Singapore, he's married twelve years. He married a woman in Taiwan when he went there to study Chinese. He graduated from school and they kept in touch and eventually he got a job in Taiwan and they decided to get married. We went over for the wedding, and I remember she [said] to me that my son would not be the proper Chinese father because he was too laid back and easy going. Her father had been very stern. So she's the disciplinarian and he's the Mommy-type.

They're very good parents. She's a wonderful mother, very involved in the life of her children. They are very obedient, but not downtrodden, and it's fun to see the Asian way of raising children which is very quiet, very effective. She's always in charge of their food, she nursed them until they were 18 months old. The boy is eight and the girl is five. She gives them little bites of things, they never eat between meals. No snacks, no going to the refrigerator and looking in. The opposite of [how] my daughter's children are being raised. I never hear her raise her voice, it's just not done.

The children are in a private American overseas school with many nationalities, and they speak English in the school. But their mother always speaks to them in Mandarin. My son speaks to them in English. And more and more they want to speak English and this is a sadness for her. She wants them to be able to read and write and speak Mandarin. I think they will. They were born in Hong Kong, so to them English is a second language.

My son worked in New York for two years after college, then he went to Taiwan. I don't think they're permanent in Singapore, maybe they will come back. He works for Bank of America. He's in Mergers and Acquisitions, M and A, and he knows lots of people in the Far East, he's valuable to them. I don't know what he would do here.

Discipline? There's no hitting. For punishment in my daughter's home, there's only time out, go to your room. With American parents, authority is eroding, yes, it's true, children lack respect. But with my son's children, I am amazed, I mean they know who's boss. I don't see them very often, but my son is very good at telling stories, and they obey. An old fashioned word, obey. I am amazed at how much they obey. Being raised in this mixed milieu, it's fascinating. I think they show great respect for their parents. Less so in my daughter's home.

My son's wife, it is she who is the disciplinarian, she is…Oh my gosh, I wish I knew the right word, she knows an enormous amount about children, that was her field, Early Childhood. She has a Master's in it and she will advise my son. They went together three years [because] one or the other wouldn't commit, and finally they did. No, it doesn't disturb me that my grandchildren are mixed. I don't know if her mother objected, it wasn't discussed. I think it must have been happy for [my daughter-in-law] because she was marrying someone who had a lot more money than she was ever capable of making. She came from a really poor family, her father was a laborer in Taiwan. She is the oldest of six and she had to work when she was in school. She's a very smart woman and they're talking about possibly coming back her.

Was I broken hearted that my grandchildren would live in Singapore? I try not to think about it. This sounds Pollyannaish, my chief concern is that my son be happy with his wife and children. Oh, I'm going to cry. When I see him and say goodbye each year, I get teary-eyed. It's really something I have pushed aside.

I have so many friends whose kids married a person of a different culture or ethnic origin. That's the way the world is going. And judging from the current census, I think it's exciting. No, it doesn't bother me at all. I have two Korean nephews who are adopted. I think the world is getting more used to it.

We mostly speak on the phone, write letters, that stuff. I would like to be close to them, like the bond with my daughter's children. But I'm not really close to them. They're put on the phone, and they *dutifully* speak to me and to their grandfather. He's called *Agong*, I think it means grandpa. No, we don't videotape, we send photos occasionally.

Birthdays? That's a problem. It's a problem for me to know how to treat their birthdays. Because I never get a thank-you, it's not done in the Chinese culture. Maybe five months later someone will say, 'By the way…' I get a sense [that] birthdays are not a big deal. Well, I do send something, but I do it grudgingly, not being sure I'm sending the right gift. And the whole thing…well, I don't know where I fit in. In Singapore, their parents don't want them to have everything. They're rather frugal and tied to a fairly simple lifestyle. The best thing I ever gave them was the last Harry Potter book and my grandson adored it, he read it over and over. I understand he's interested in tennis, so I'll try to get him a book about tennis. They love books, and I love books, so that'll be it.

It costs an arm and a leg to send things to Singapore. Videos? Oh, that's a big story in Singapore. You know it's a dictatorship. I used to send videos thinking that was the perfect gift, until my son told me he had to go down to the customs office, and he had to describe in detail what the video was, and then pay them to view it and decide whether or not it could stay in Singapore. So that seems like a lot of work. I'm not going to send any more videos.

I send letters. But I haven't gotten any answers, so I figured it's too much time for them. So the best thing is to talk on the phone. We talk about every ten days, every two weeks. My son's very good about calling. His wife in person is quite reticent, but on the phone she's ebullient, she's wonderful.

I think she's frightened of me. I try to be friendly and nice, but I guess it's so much part of their culture that they fear the mother-in-law. Oh, yes, it's terrible. When a Chinese girl—I think it's still true in Taiwan—[when] she marries, she goes to live in the home of her husband, and her mother-in-law is her boss. In some cases, it's very cruel, she's almost like a servant in the house. It's a terrible system and it's age old. I'm hoping that as her kids get older and more independent, we can chat. I'd love to talk to her, but that's been hard to do, hard to overcome.

My son and daughter are planning a vacation for the whole family this year. And I think eventually, [they] might return in two, three years. It's partly my fault we're not closer to the grandchildren because I don't do e-mail, that kind of stuff. We could visit more frequently, [but] it's an arduous trip, 24 hours door-to-door. You know, I'm 67. I would only do it again if I could fly business class. It's very expensive.

We went to see them four times. We went to Hong Kong, and we traveled to Thailand on a little vacation with them. And to Taiwan. The trips were three weeks. But that was *before* they were married. We've gone twice since the grandchildren.

Tips for long-distance grandparents? Boy, I don't know. I wish people would give me some tips. Everybody's different. [With] my daughter-in-law, that's always a touchy situation. A completely different country makes the [relationship] a little uncertain for me, and I guess for her too.

I don't complain to my son. I don't think my life is of particular interest to them or to those little kids. I'm their grandmother, that's true. But I think this tie that we all have to Vermont is very strong. My son has said he'd like to send his kids to camp in the United States, but they're not ready for it yet.

I'm sure there's a lot more I could be doing, and I probably feel guilty that I'm not. But as they get older, my ability to communicate with them will be better, will be easier. I send them gifts, not many, but some, and they know who I am. And I see them every summer in Vermont. [For] a week or ten days, we are together. And the kids love it there. There's a little cabin that they stay in, and a cabin we stay in, and there's all kinds of back and forth. It's very informal, swimming and boating.

Most of the fun revolves around eating, sitting around the table. Just going to the beach and throwing rocks in the water, fishing, they adore fishing. And sawing wood and running around. As a long-distance grandmother, I keep in touch mostly by phone.

The best part of being a grandmother happened when my first grandchild was born. I remember thinking *This is a cosmic experience.* When you think about it, it's a lot of fun to be a grandparent. I'm amazed at how much I do like to play with them. The fun of being a kid again, and seeing it through their eyes.

The most difficult part is standing by [when] you see something being done in a way you don't approve of [and] you hold your tongue. I tiptoe more around my son. I would be very reluctant to say anything about his wife, whereas I wouldn't be reluctant to say something about my daughter's husband. I'm more careful with my son."

SMART TIPS FROM CHRISTINE

Marrying a person of a different race or culture is the way the world is going.

Be pleased that your child is happy with their spouse and children.

Try not to be broken hearted because your grandchildren live far away.

Expect to be sad and get teary-eyed each time you say goodbye to them.

Send letters and photos to them, and call them frequently.

Even if your grandchildren are put on the phone and speak dutifully, continue to call.

Send your grandchildren birthday gifts even if you don't get a thank-you note or an acknowledgement.

Buy them appropriate books according to their interests, like tennis or Harry Potter.

Keep sending letters, even if you don't get an answer.

If your grandchildren live in another country and speak another language, try to overcome the barriers.

Understand the customs of that country, and pay attention to their rules.

Travel to their location to visit them and take them on a family vacation.

Have them visit you, and include all the siblings and cousins.

If you don't do email, find other ways to keep in touch.

Don't complain to your child about his spouse or your grandchildren.

In long distance grandparenting, tip toe around and be sensitive to your child's spouse.

Despite distance and different cultures, enjoy the small pleasures whenever you are with your grandchildren.

A yearly family vacation together is a wonderful way to stay close.

Christine's relationships to her grandchildren are very different. Because her daughter is her neighbor, she sees those grandkids on a casual, almost daily basis. It's pretty easygoing, it's very close, and it's extremely rewarding.

Vastly different is her relationship to her son's children who live half way around the world. Her relationship to these grandkids is frustrating because distance, language, and cultures separate them. Although they speak on the phone and see each other in Vermont each summer, it's difficult to maintain closeness. Her son's wife is Asian and her native language is Mandarin. Clearly, her relationship to these grand-kids can not approach the closeness she has with her daughter's kids.

You can feel her anger in sending videos that require approval by the Singapore customs officials, letters that go unanswered, and gifts that are not acknowledged. Still, she tries hard to overcome these obstacles.

Christine's story tells you what it feels like being a long-distance grandparent and the hardships you need to overcome. Today, many families are separated by miles and time zones and countries. By language and culture as well. Long distance grandparenting is a major challenge and **Christine** shows us that it can be done.

In the final chapter, we take a wide angle look at what these ten grandparents have shared. You've read stories of pain and stories of joy. Tragedies that have no solution, and achievements that deserve applause. Yes, grandparenting today takes on many forms!

12

SUMMING UP

Now that you've read the intimate stories of these ten grandparents who became **THE EXTRA PARENT**, what do you think? Take time out to review them. Was there *one* story that really spoke to you? Did you find a particular *part* of a story that touched you? What was your reaction to the **SMART TIPS** that each grandparent offered? Did you disagree with some of them? What are your reasons? If you were in their shoes, what would you have done?

In Chapter 7, we saw **KEISHA** struggling with poverty, prostitution, and drug abuse. However, now she is raising four grandchildren, holding down a part-time job, and desperately trying to earn a college degree. That's Keisha's experience.

What a difference it is from **CHRISTINE'S** experience, in Chapter 11. At age 67, she lives on an elegant four acre estate, flies to Singapore, and spends summer vacations with her grandkids in adjoining cabins in Vermont.

Every grandparent's experience is unique.

Many **factors** affect the way we interact with our grandchildren. What are they?

It would be easy to conclude that **money** (or lack of it) is the major factor that determines your relationship to your grandkids. Yes, money is a weighty factor, but not necessarily the most important one. Take **ALICE,** in Chapter 2. She had serious financial problems, yet she managed to keep her family together on a tight budget. Money counts, but there are other important factors. Let's look at them.

The **age** of the grandparent is another factor. **ALICE,** in her forties, is our youngest grandmother, while **JUDY** is a step-grandmother in her eighties. Four decades make a huge difference. A young grandparent, blessed with energy and health, will have more ability to cope than an elderly grandparent who is facing illnesses and diminishing earning power. Remember **SARAH** in Chapter 4? In her seventies, she is still raising a grandson and taking care of a sick husband in his eighties. Becoming **THE EXTRA PARENT** is considerably easier if you're younger.

Another factor is the **distance** between the grandparent's home and the grandchildren's. Some grandparents have only a short trip to see their grandchildren. They can take a bus, hop a train, or drive over, so staying close is not a problem. Both **BETTY**, in Chapter 3, and **DAVID**, in Chapter 9, drove to their grandchildren's home several times a week. And **MARILYN**, in Chapter 10, stopped by her grandchildren's house almost every day. Living in the next town or nearby makes it a lot easier.

Sadly, three grandmothers were *forced* by tragedy to take on the responsibilities of **THE EXTRA PARENT**, *forced* to raise their grandchildren because their child couldn't do it. **SARAH,** for example, had to raise her infant grandson because her daughter died, and **ALICE** took over when her daughter became pregnant out of wedlock. They did not choose these roles. A crisis propelled them into it. **Crisis** or **choice** are important factors that influence the grandparenting relationship. If the job was forced on them, they are likely to feel anger and resentment. But a grandparent who chooses to help out is likely to be having a wonderful time.

Home ownership is another important factor. When **ALICE** took on the parenting role, it was in *her* house, she was the owner. And **JUAN-ITA,** in Chapter 8, was the owner of *her* house. Each grandmother got financial and emotional support from her husband. She was not doing the job all alone, and she was not living under the roof of a child who looked upon her as a burden. **Home ownership** is another factor that colors the relationship. It confers respect and authority.

Power and **discipline** are other factors that may be determined by who owns the home that the three generations occupy. Who is the boss? Who sets the rules? Who doles out punishments and rewards? Three generations living together under the same roof have to hammer out these issues and make decisions about wielding power and imposing discipline.

Cultural background determines family values and is another factor in the grandparenting relationship. In **LIN'S** three generation household, although he is Christian, his granddaughters are being raised Chinese, and the parents insist they must study Mandarin. For **BETTY** and **MARILYN,** enriching their grandchildren by taking them to cultural events, like museums and theatres, gives them great satisfaction.

Of course, no three-generation family is free of stress. But the **attitude** the grandparent has toward stress is a large factor in the relationship. Every grandparent faces obstacles and makes choices about how to manage stress. **ALICE'S** attitude was upbeat and optimistic and her sunny nature contributed to her family's success. She really listened to her grandson, she enjoyed fun activities with him, and she was a role model for being a team player. Her **attitude** played a large role in the well being of her family.

For some grandparents, **religion** was a strong factor and it provided them with great comfort and strength. For **ALICE** and **KEISHA** and **SARAH**, that was certainly true. But for **DAVID** and **JUANITA,** religion played only a minor role. What mattered to them was passing on the **ethical values** they cherished.

Okay, let's make a list. What factors influence grandparents who become **THE EXTRA PARENT**? Every grandparent expressed **Love.** Deep love. Abiding love. Unending love. Even those forced into terrible situations and faced with tremendous hardships spoke of how dear and how sweet the attachment was. So let's begin our list with the number one factor **Love.** However, if our list of factors doesn't feel comprehensive to you, write down your own ideas on the blank page at the end of this book.

Factors That Influence
the Grandparenting Relationship

Love

Money

Age

Distance

Crisis or Choice

Home Ownership

Power and Discipline

Cultural Background

Attitude

Religion or Ethical Values

This book makes no claim for statistical or sociological analysis. What we've gathered is slices of oral history, the kind of truth you feel right down to the tips of your toes. The ten grandparents you read about are not meant to suggest that all grandparents fall into these categories. However, many grandparents share the same conflicts and challenges. The **SMART TIPS** each grandparent offers at the end of each chapter can help you understand your own grandparenting experience. Their stories assure you that you're not alone.

Today, grandparents are living longer and healthier lives. Many are in better financial shape than they ever expected. Grandparents are also a growing political and economic force in America. Their opinions deserve to be heard and their contributions to society should be celebrated. Perhaps no contribution is more valuable than the grandparenting connection.

Becoming **THE EXTRA PAERNT** could turn out to be one of most satisfying experiences of your life. People love to tell stories about the wonderful times they had with their grandparents. *Funny* stories. *Poignant* stories. *Important* stories. These stories carry a message and often they become part of the family's history. As grandparents, you are making these stories happen.

Perhaps one day *your* grandchildren will be telling stories to *their* grandchildren. How special you were to them. How much they loved you. What a vital role you played in shaping their life.

Finally...

Each grandparent who appeared in this book gave generously of their time. Their interview was taped, transcribed, and edited. You have read their exact words. Their names have been changed to provide anonymity.

In 1997, about 7.7 % of all kids in the USA (5,435,000) were living in homes with a grandparent. But huge numbers of grandparents who take care of their grandchildren don't live with them. These are hidden numbers that the Census Bureau doesn't report.

Many grandparents in their fifties and sixties are still holding down jobs.

A 1998 AARP Grandparenting Survey suggests that 11% of mature grandparents are caregivers. About 80% of them are grandmothers.

By the year 2050, if current trends continue, the population of people over 65 will grow by 135% (AARP, 1998).

Over the past 25 years, the number of children being raised by someone other than their parents has increased dramatically.

THE EXTRA PARENT crosses sociological, economic, and ethnic groups.

Resources and Organizations

AARP Grandparent Information Center
601 E Street NW
Washington, D.C. 20049
202-434-2296

Generations United
122 C Street NW Suite 820
Washington, D.C. 20001
202-638-1263

Grandparents United
137 Larkin St.
Madison WI 53705
904-223-0559

The Brookdale Center on Aging
425 East 25 St. 13 fl
New York, NY 10010
212-481-3780

Kinship Care Program of Child Welfare League of America
50 F St. NW 6 fl
Washington, D.C. 20001
202-942-0324

Family Friends Resource Center
The National Council on the Aging
300 D St. SW 8 fl
Washington, D.C. 20024
202-479-6672

The Jewish Board of Family and Children's Services
120 West 57th St.
New York, NY 10019
212-632-4760

Also check your phone book for local and state Offices on Aging.

Bibliography for Further Reading

Brown, Ruth Meyer. *A Grandmother's Guide to Extended Babysitting*. Sterling, VA: Capital Books, 2001.

Carson, Lillian. *The Essential Grandparent: A Guide to Making a Difference*. Deerfield Beach, FL: Health Communications, 1996.

Ciardi, Charmaine L., Cathy Nikkel Orme, and Carolyn Quatrano. *The Magic of Grandparenting*. New York: Henry Holt, 1995.

Cohen, Joan Schrager. *Helping Your Grandchildren Through Their Parents' Divorce*. New York: Walker and Company, 1994.

Dalton, Rosemary, and Peter Dalton. *The Encyclopedia of Grandparenting*. San Leandro, CA: Bristol Publishing, 1990.

Furstenberg, F., and A. Cherlin. *Divided Families*. Cambridge, MA: Harvard University Press. Generations United, Washington, DC, 1992.

Kitzinger, Sheila. *Becoming A Grandmother: A Life Transition*. New York: Scribner, 1996.

Kornhaber, Arthur, M.D. *The Grandparent Guide: The Definitive Guide to Coping with the Challenges of Modern Grandparenting*. Chicago: Contemporary Books, 2002.

Le Shan, Eda. *Grandparenting in a Changing World*. New York: Newmarket Press, 1993.

Takas, Marianne. *Relatives Raising Children*. New York: Brookdale Foundation Group, 1998.

Westheimer, Ruth, and Pierre Lehu. *Dr. Ruth Talks about Grandparents: Advice for Kids on Making the Most of a Special Relationship*. New York: Farrar Strauss & Giroux, 1997.

Westheimer, Dr. Ruth, and Dr. Steven Kaplan. *Grandparenthood*. New York: Routledge, 1998.

Notes

About the Author

Elaine Denholtz is an award-winning journalist, playwright, and screenwriter who has written six non-fiction books and appeared on over 100 TV and radio talk shows across the country. A member of Phi Beta Kappa and The New Jersey Literary Hall of Fame, she teaches at Fairleigh Dickinson University.

0-595-30400-1